Travels with my paintbrush

Grace T McKee

DEDICATION

For Phillip who strongly supports me in my painting ventures, accompanies me on my travels (carrying all my heavy painting supplies), and is also my most truthful critic!   I value his opinion greatly, especially as he is not afraid of calling a spade a spade.

CONTENTS

ACKNOWLEDGMENTS

I am deeply grateful to all the art instructors whose workshops I have attended for giving generously of their time and knowledge in order that their students might learn and improve.

Introduction

Painting is my passion and my life. My day is not complete until I have painted at least a couple of strokes – even if it is just making changes to the painting I did the day before!

This book is intended to show the joy of painting. It is a narrative, in a way, of the pleasure experienced when beautiful scenes, objects or people are seen and reflects my intense desire to capture my feelings by transforming them into paintings.

My wanderlust led to travels in very interesting and picturesque places, all of which have a story to tell. Bright colours attract me and my paintings are therefore full of colour.

FALLING LEAVES

This painting is of a lake deep in a quiet area of France. The scene evoked feelings of mystery, moodiness and stillness. Who knows what is lurking on the far bank? Is someone watching me gaze at the autumn leaves floating on the water?

.

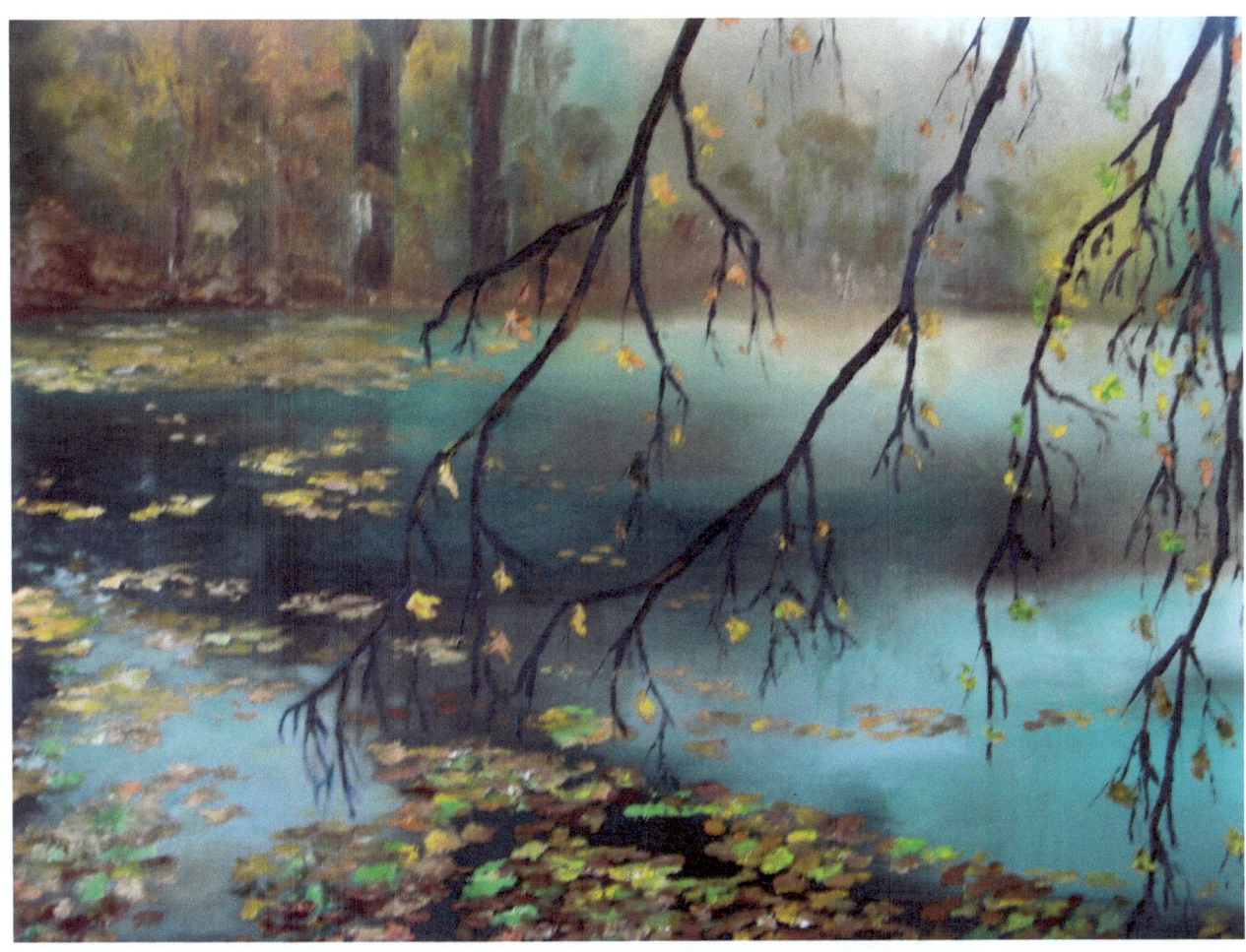

Grace T McKee

POPPIES ON A BANK

An altogether different mood is portrayed in this bright and cheerful depiction of poppies in the Deux-Sévres region of France.   These vividly coloured flowers make a wide splash of reds and orange in fields, on the verges of roads, along fences and even on walls.

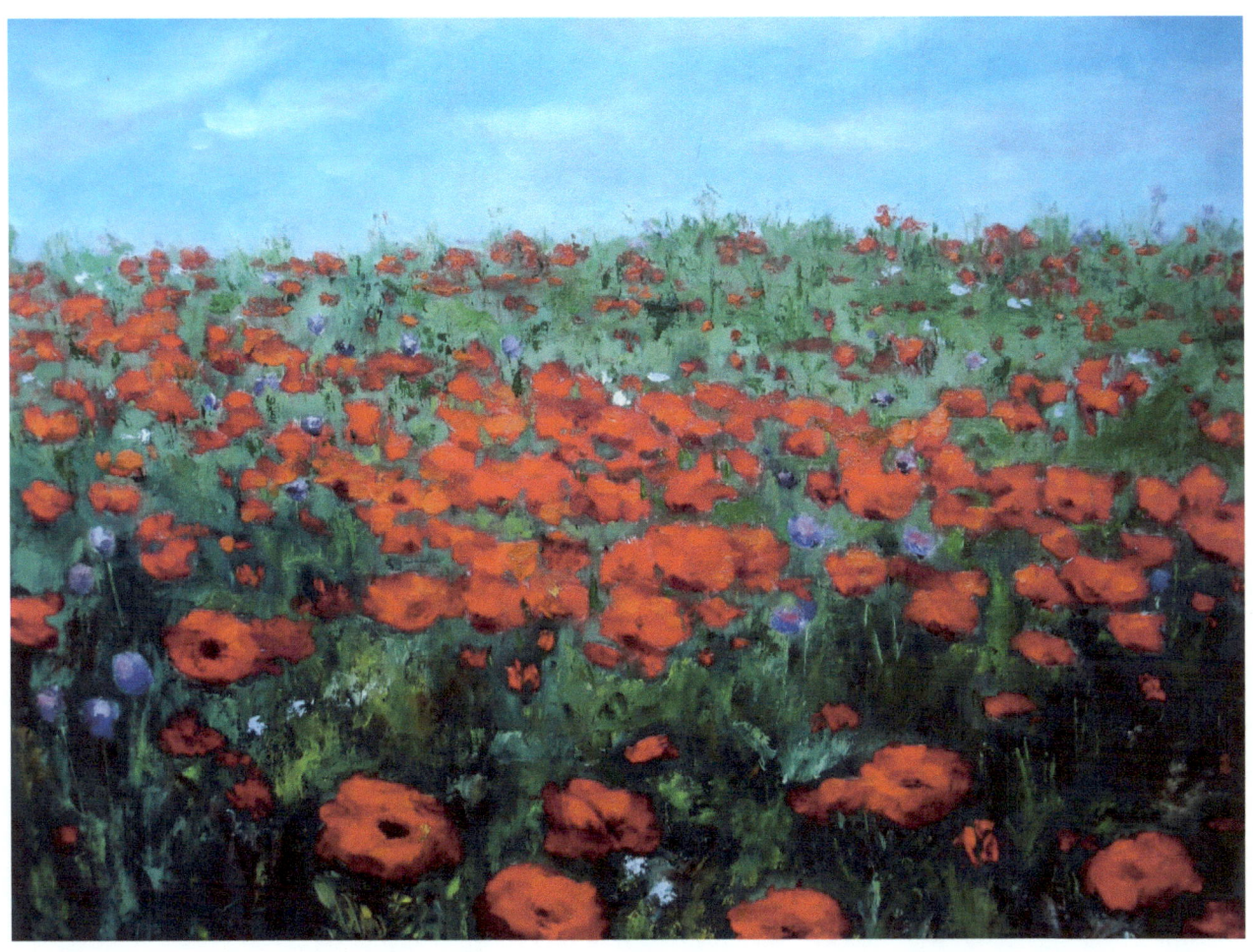

Grace T McKee

LES TOURNESOLS

Fields of sunflowers, a sea of yellow and green, with cheerful smiling faces turned towards the
sun

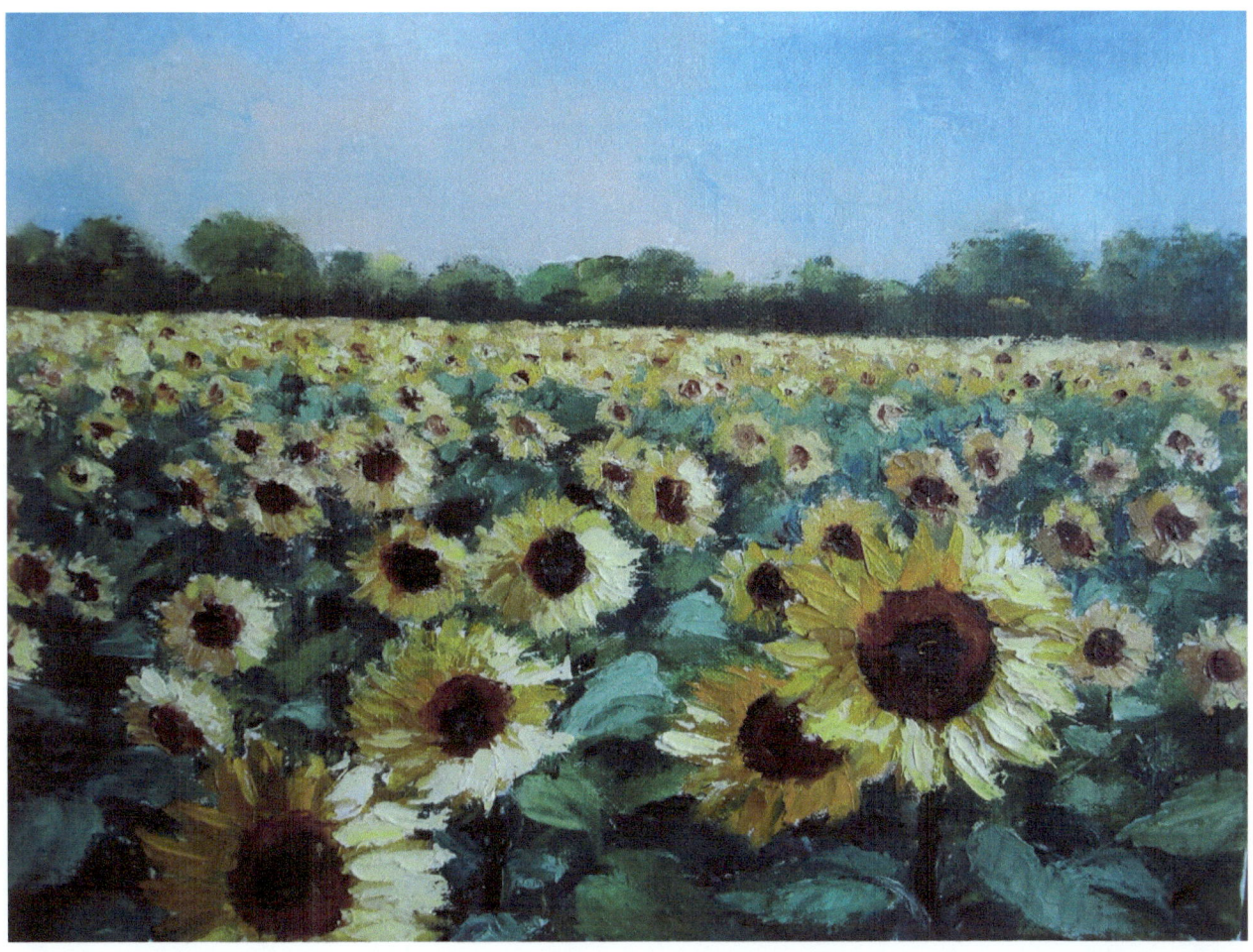

THE CHERRY ORCHARD

In spring the cherry orchards are white with blossom and one can almost hear the bees buzzing around the flowers. The branches bow heavily towards the ground, covered with masses of flowers.

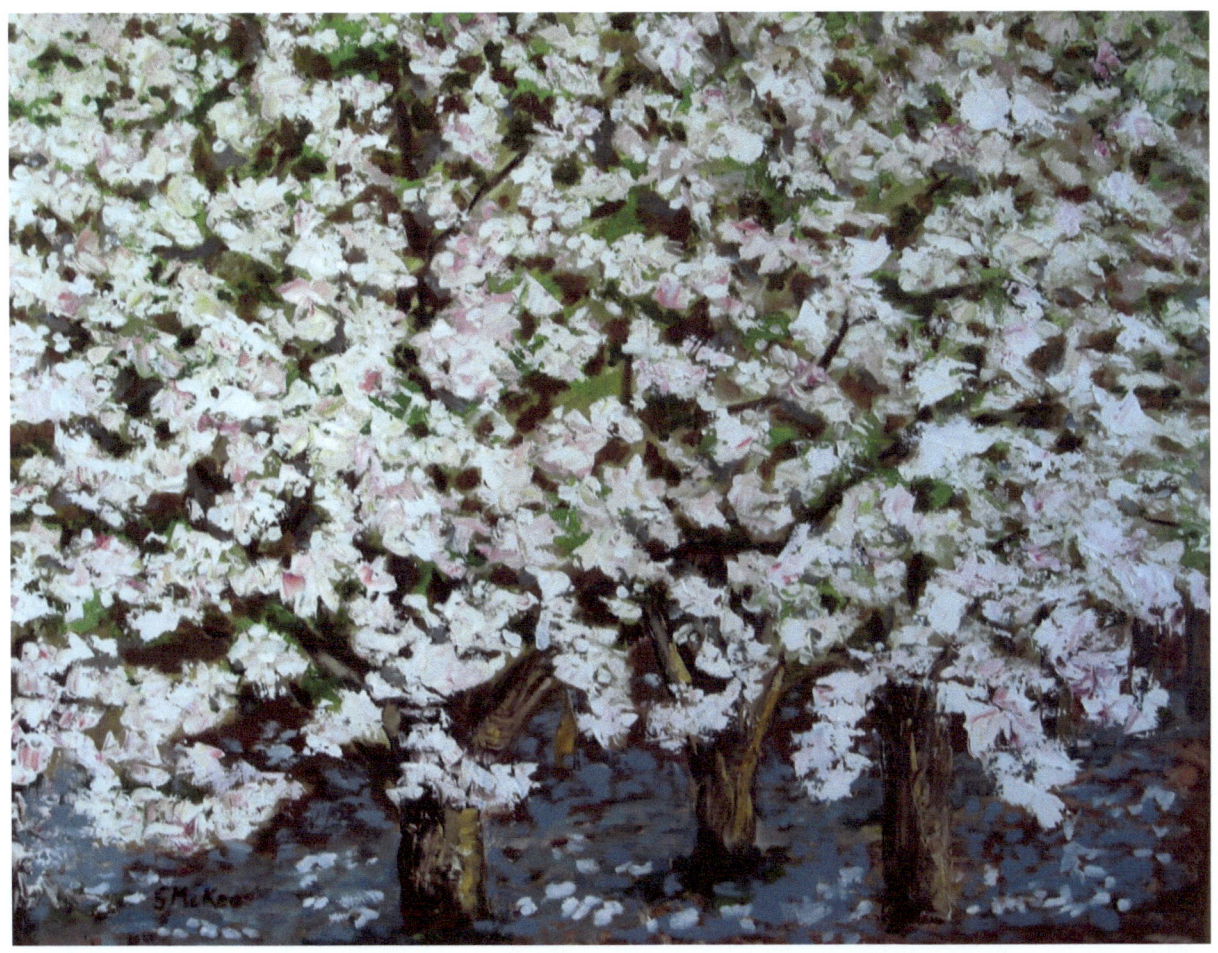

FRENCH LAVENDER

While driving through Provence one summer, we heard a low humming sound that got progressively louder as we approached the fields of lavender. They resembled a patchwork quilt in various shades of mauve, lilac and purple. It was only when we got out of the car and nearer the perfectly shaped mounds of plants that we discovered the humming sound came from the thousands of bees buzzing around the lavender flowers.

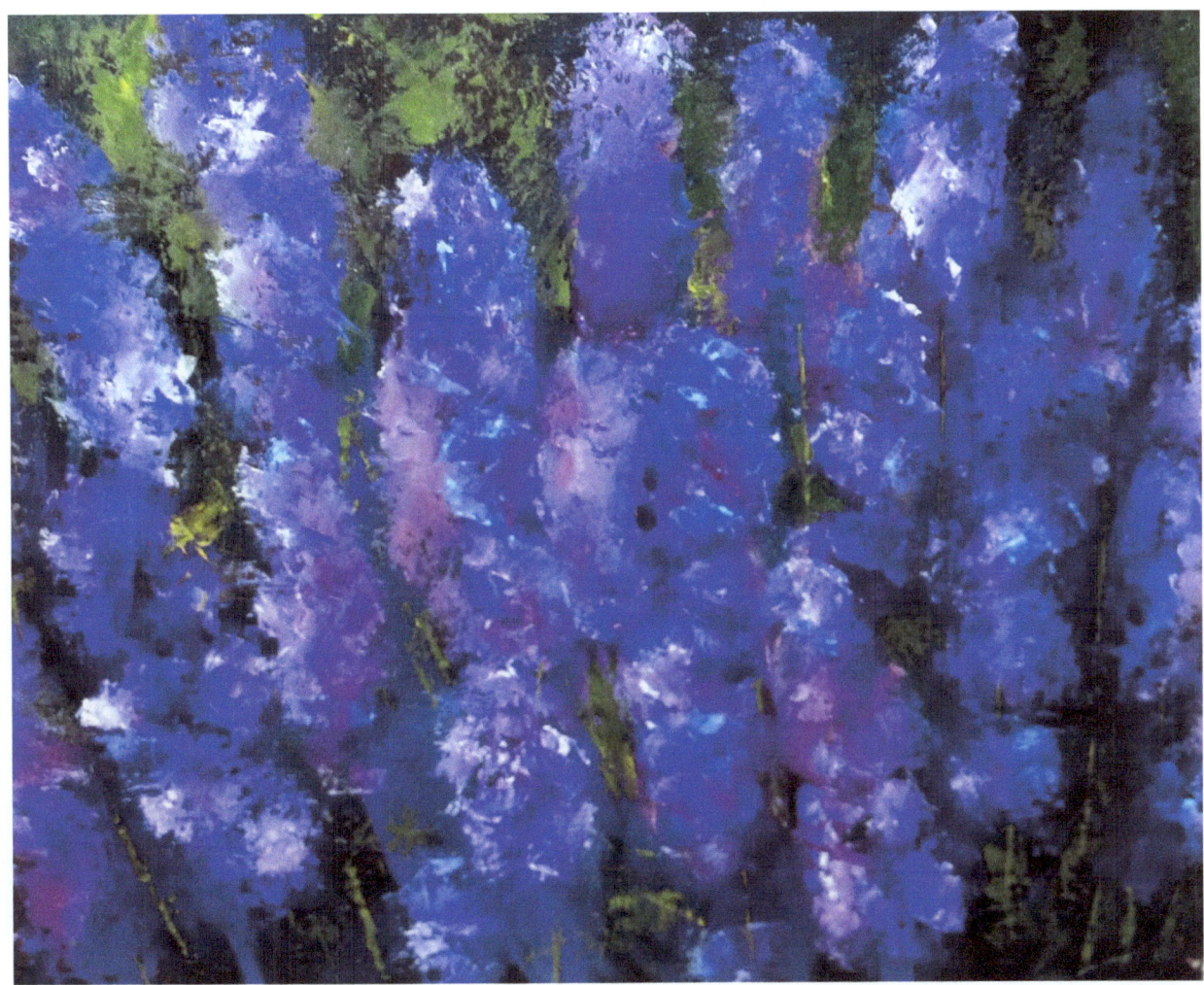

LE PRINTEMPS

In spring the trees burst forth with pale green leaves. Those lining the roads provide dappled shade for the motorists. The tranquil French countryside can be glimpsed between the elegant trees on either side.

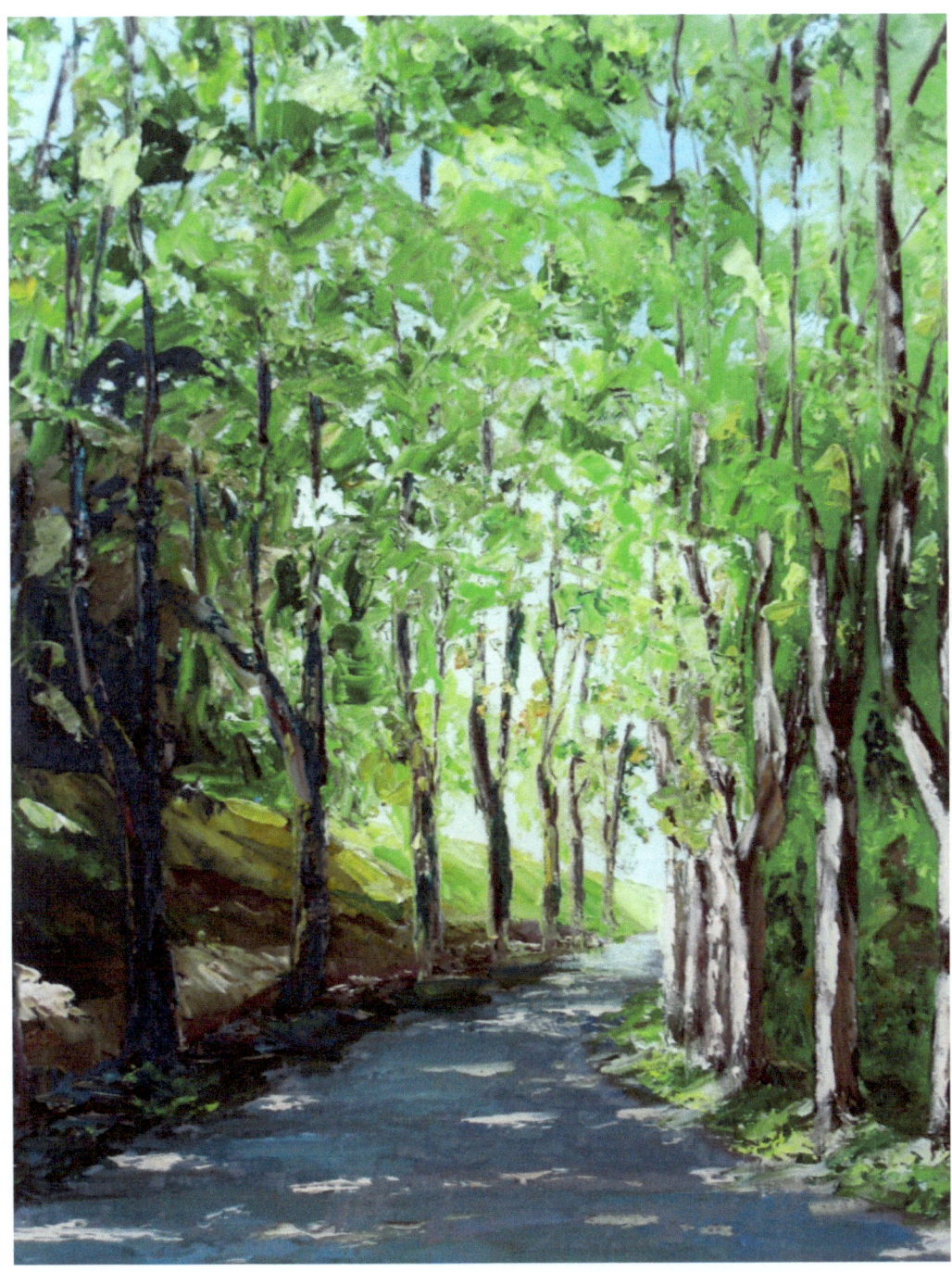

HAY BALES

I find it impossible to pass by hay bales in a field without photographing them as they make such evocative paintings. Most of the hay bales in this area are cylindrical, but I have also seen rectangular ones.

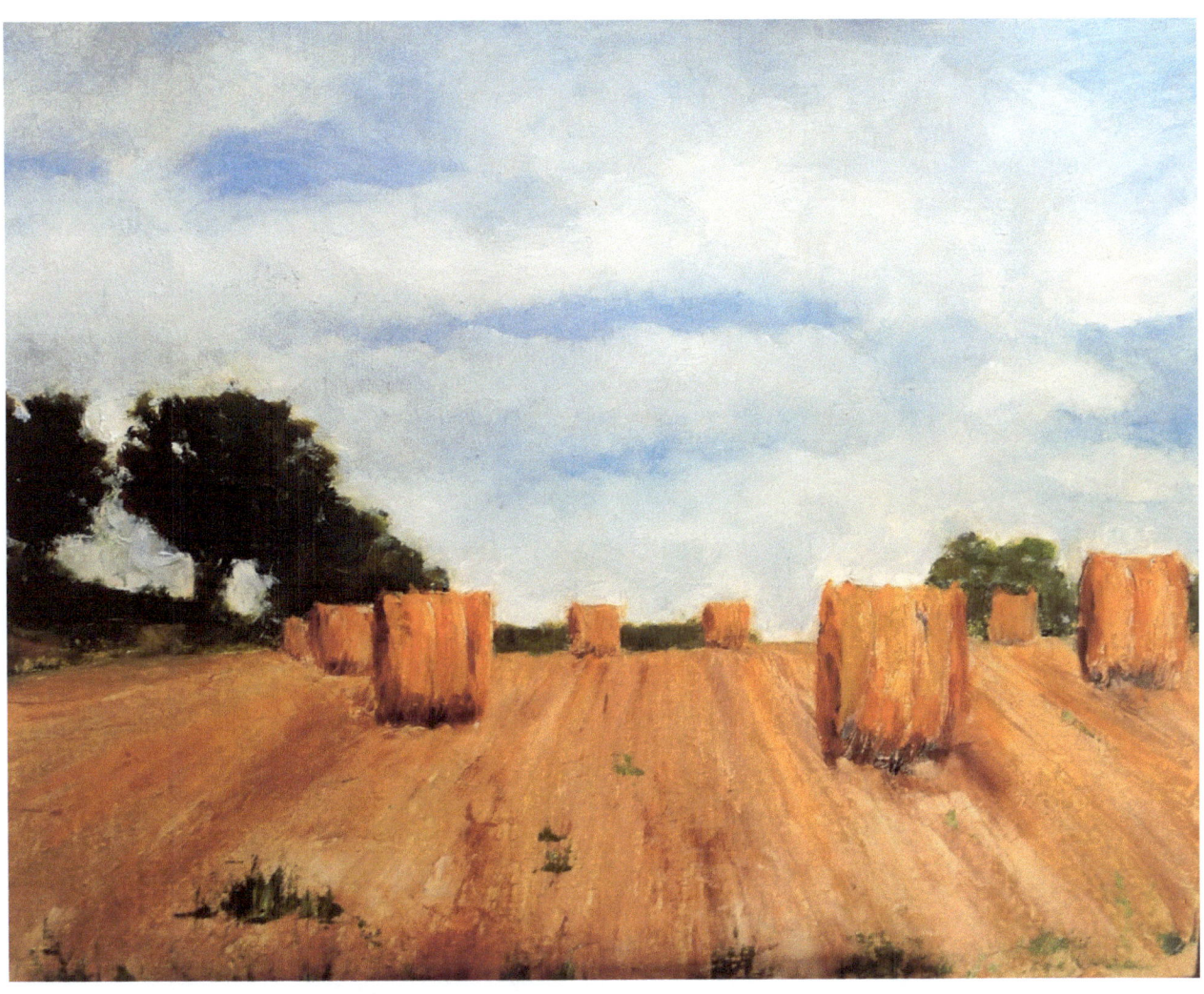

LITTLE BRIDGE IN OUCHAMPS

I saw this beautiful little green bridge over a small stream in a little village called Ouchamps, in the Loire Valley. The colour of the bridge reminded me of the one in Monet's garden and therefore deserved to be painted.

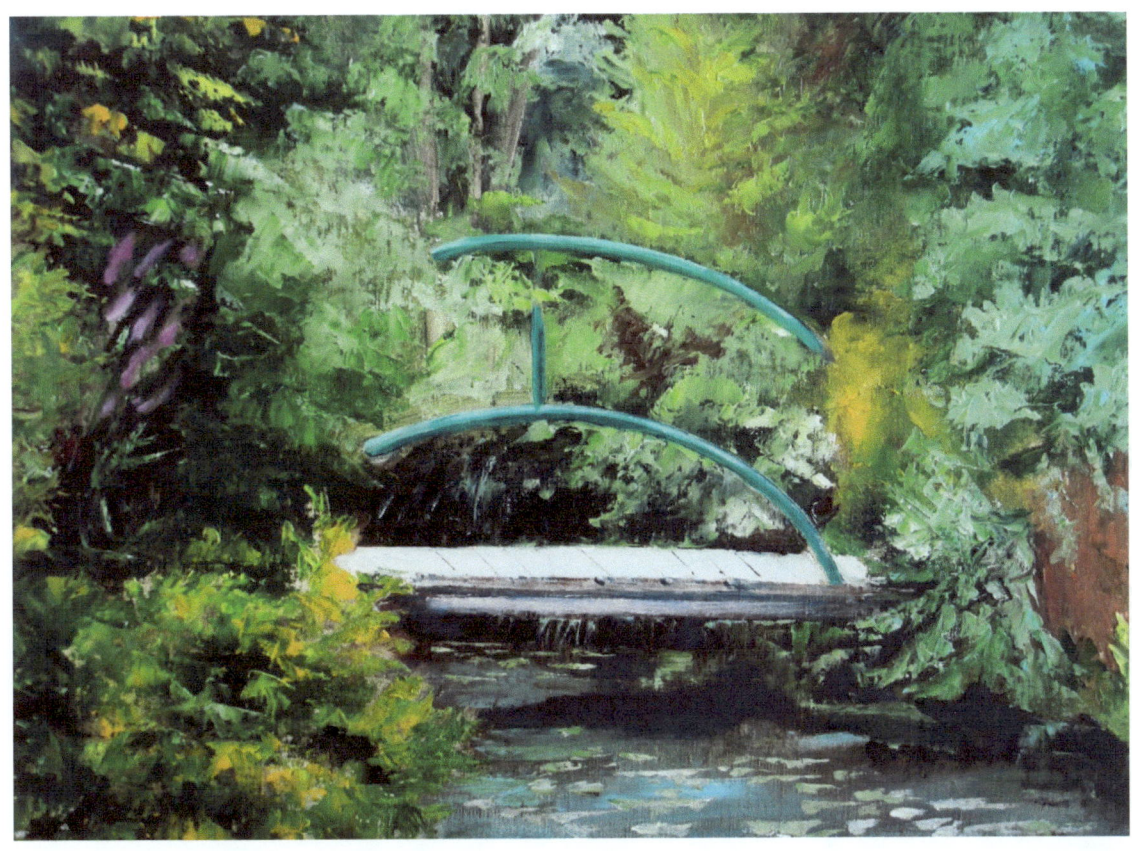

SHORN SHEEP GRAZING

A common sight in fields and meadows in France is large numbers of grazing sheep. In fact, I don't think I have seen them do anything else!

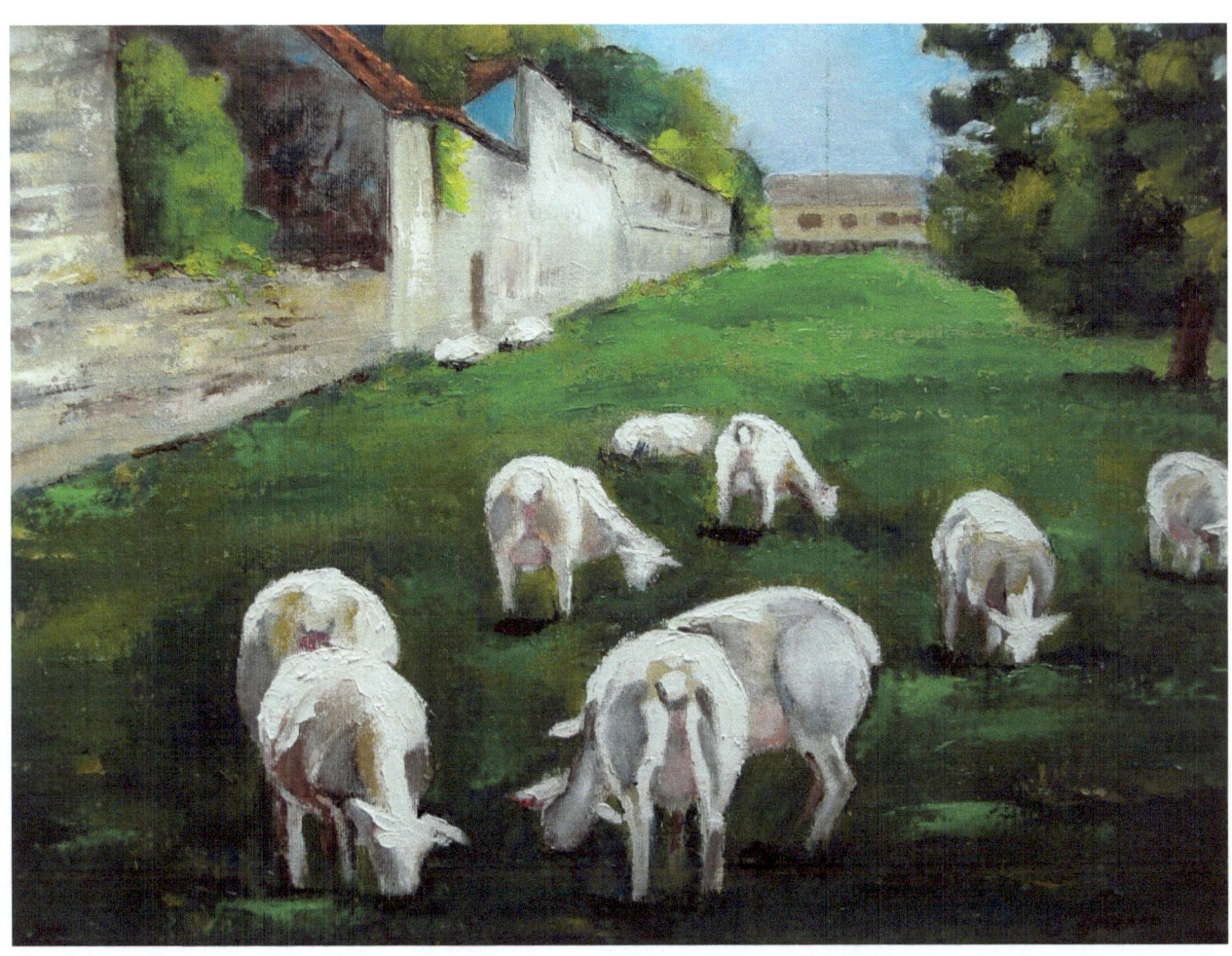

WE DON'T LIKE FOIE GRAS!

I saw these geese in a large crate in a market in the Dordogne. I thought I would give them freedom in my painting by placing them in a field.

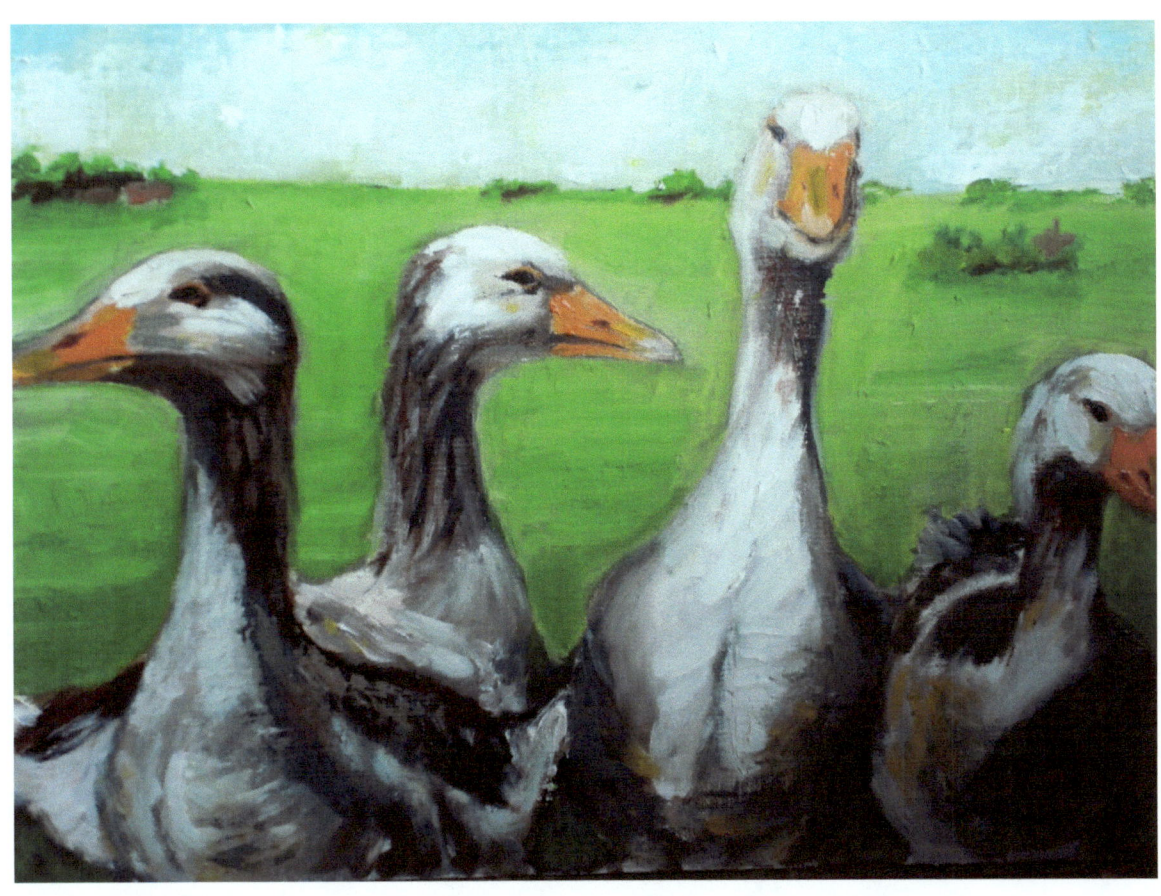

ANTELOPE CANYON

One of the most amazing places that I have ever seen! We were escorted here by a Native American guide. The colours and shapes, especially when the sun's rays shone in directly, were spectacular. Dust storms and heavy rain are not infrequent.

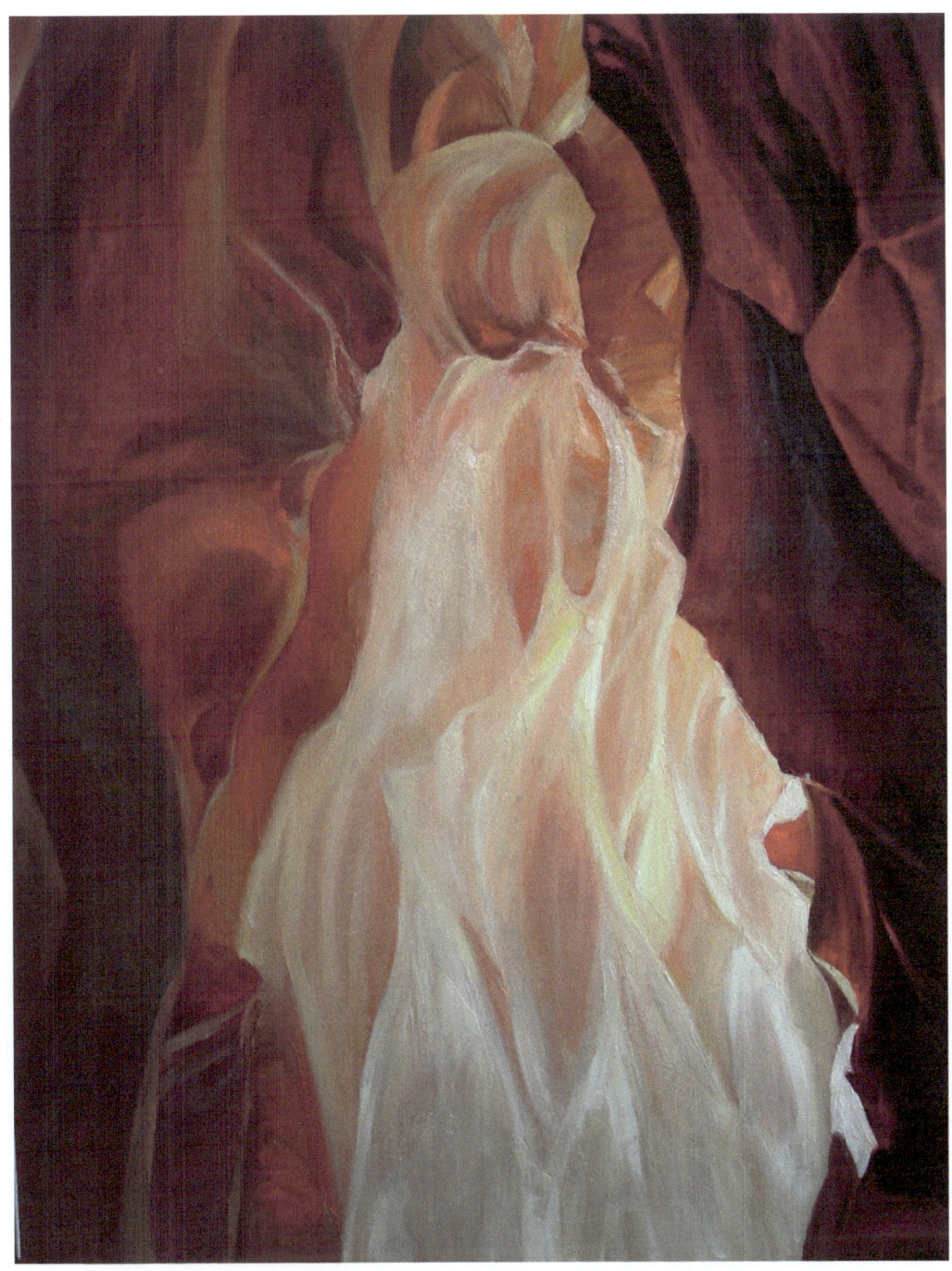

CATHEDRAL ROCK REFLECTIONS

One of the most beautiful places in the Unites States is Sedona in Arizona. The town is surrounded by amazing red rock mountains, many of which are named after their perceived shapes. Cathedral Rock is one of the better-known sites. I decided that it was more interesting to paint its reflection rather than the formation itself.

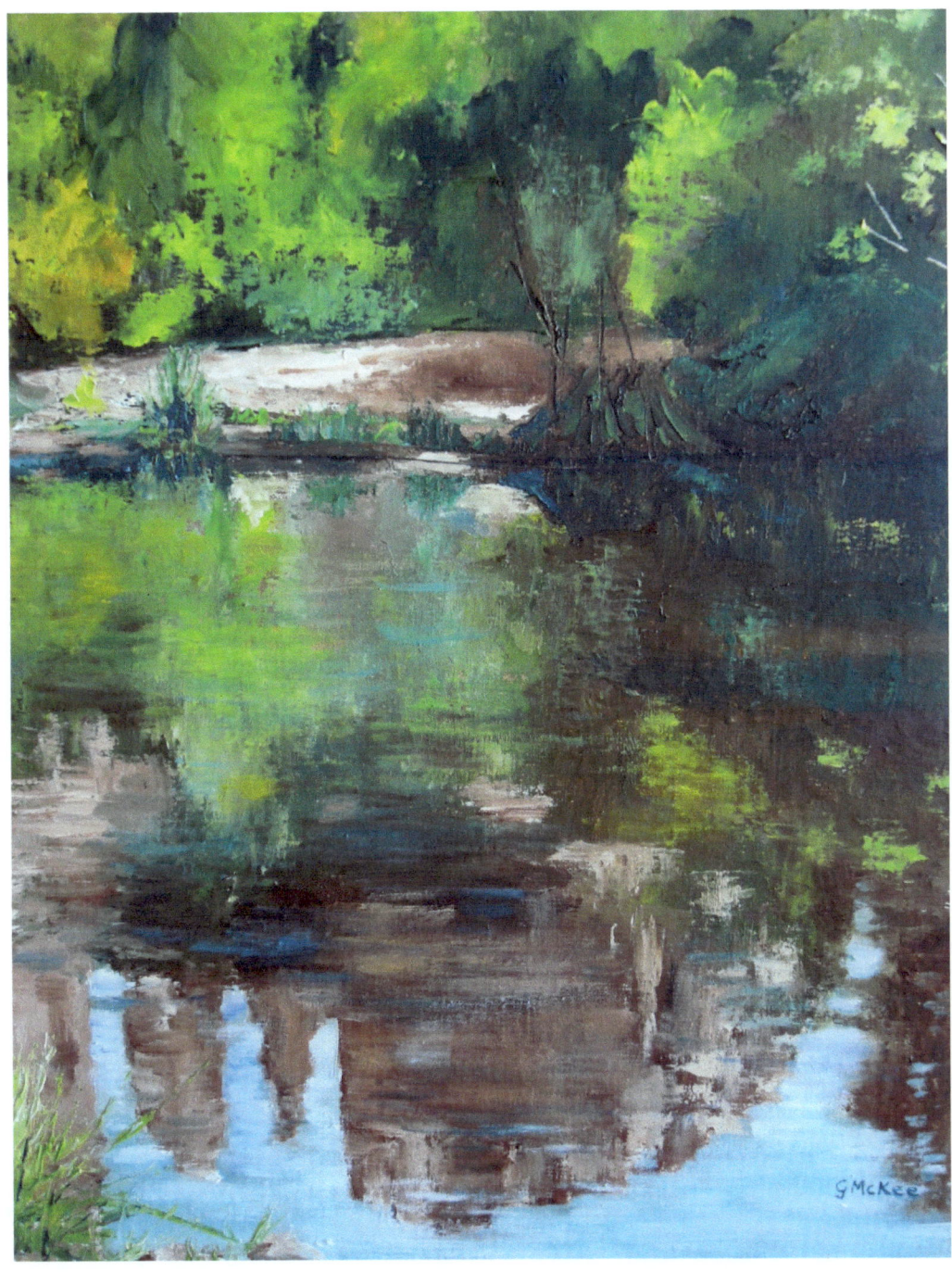

ARIZOBA LANDSCAPE

Much of Arizona is desert with its own type of beauty. This painting is of the area around Cave Creek where I used to live. Massive Saguaro cacti (over a hundred years old) and feathery palo verde trees were commonplace, as were incredibly high summer temperatures, rattlesnakes, scorpions and tarantulas!

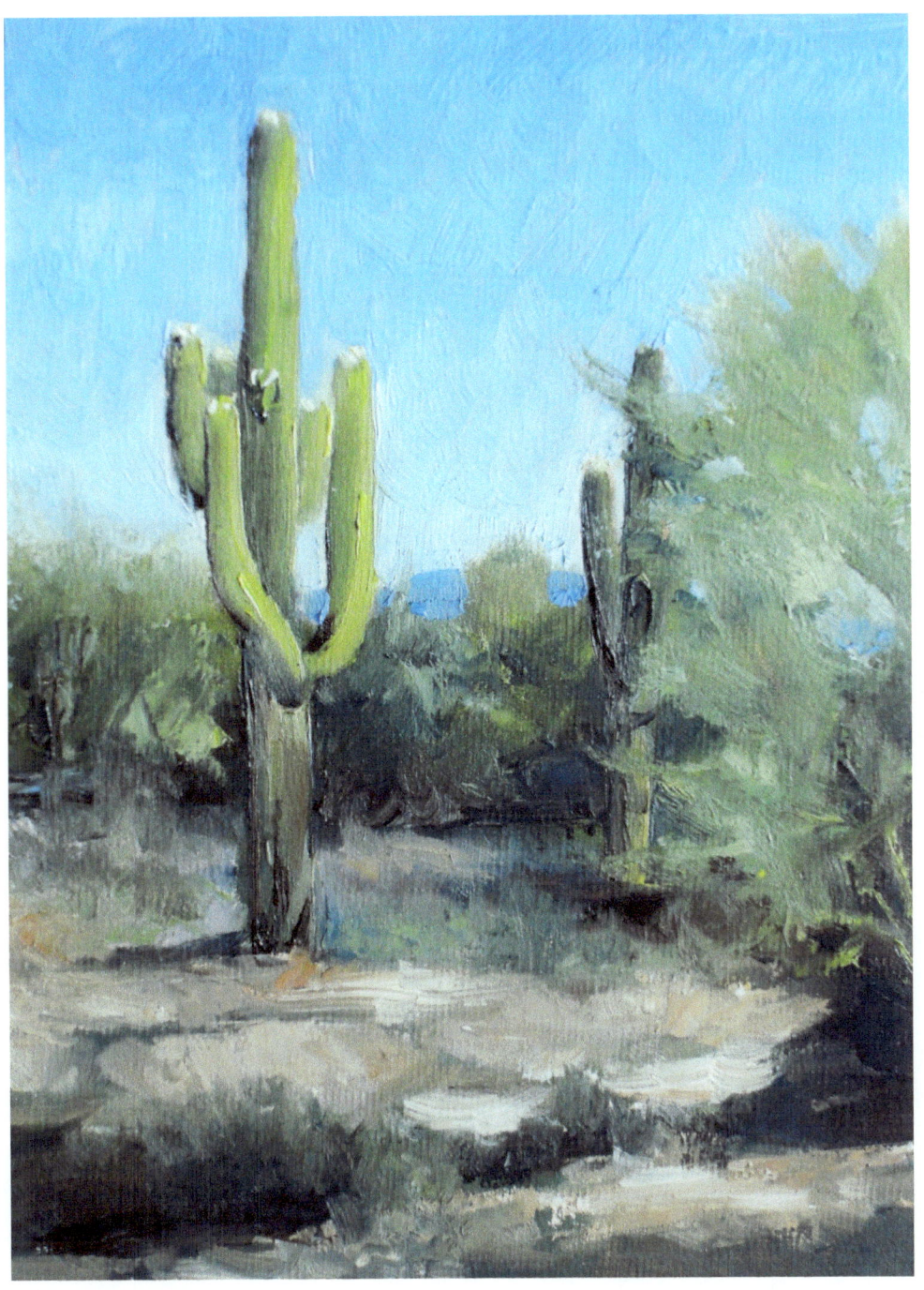

SUNSHINE AND SNOW

In contrast to the Arizona low desert, the scenery in the northeast of America is very different. Winter temperatures can be unbelievably low but on the other hand, snow scenes make beautiful paintings.

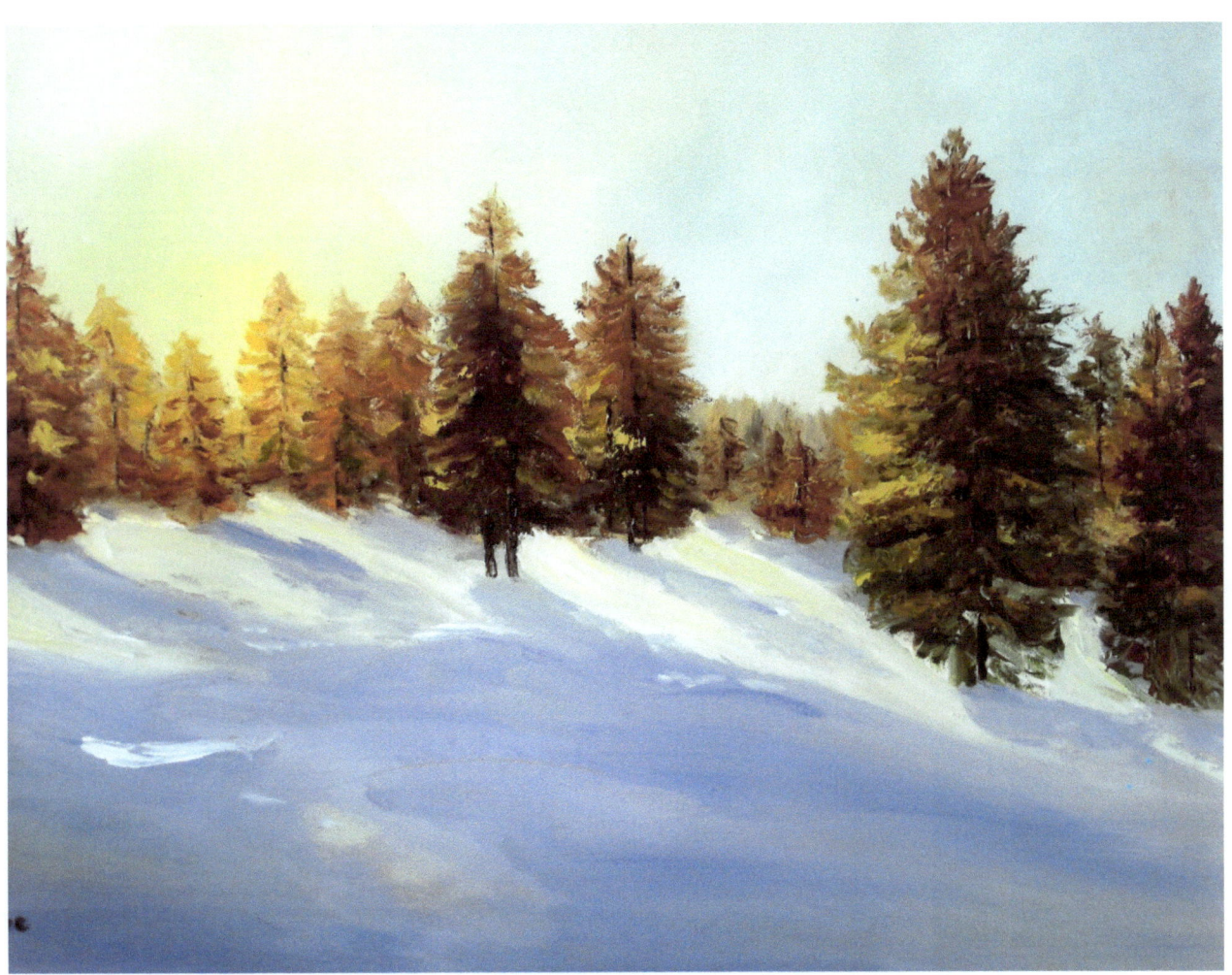

ASPENS

This painting is of an aspen grove in Colorado. These trees grow in colonies that apparently share a common root structure. I love painting aspens in the fall when their leaves are a glorious yellow.

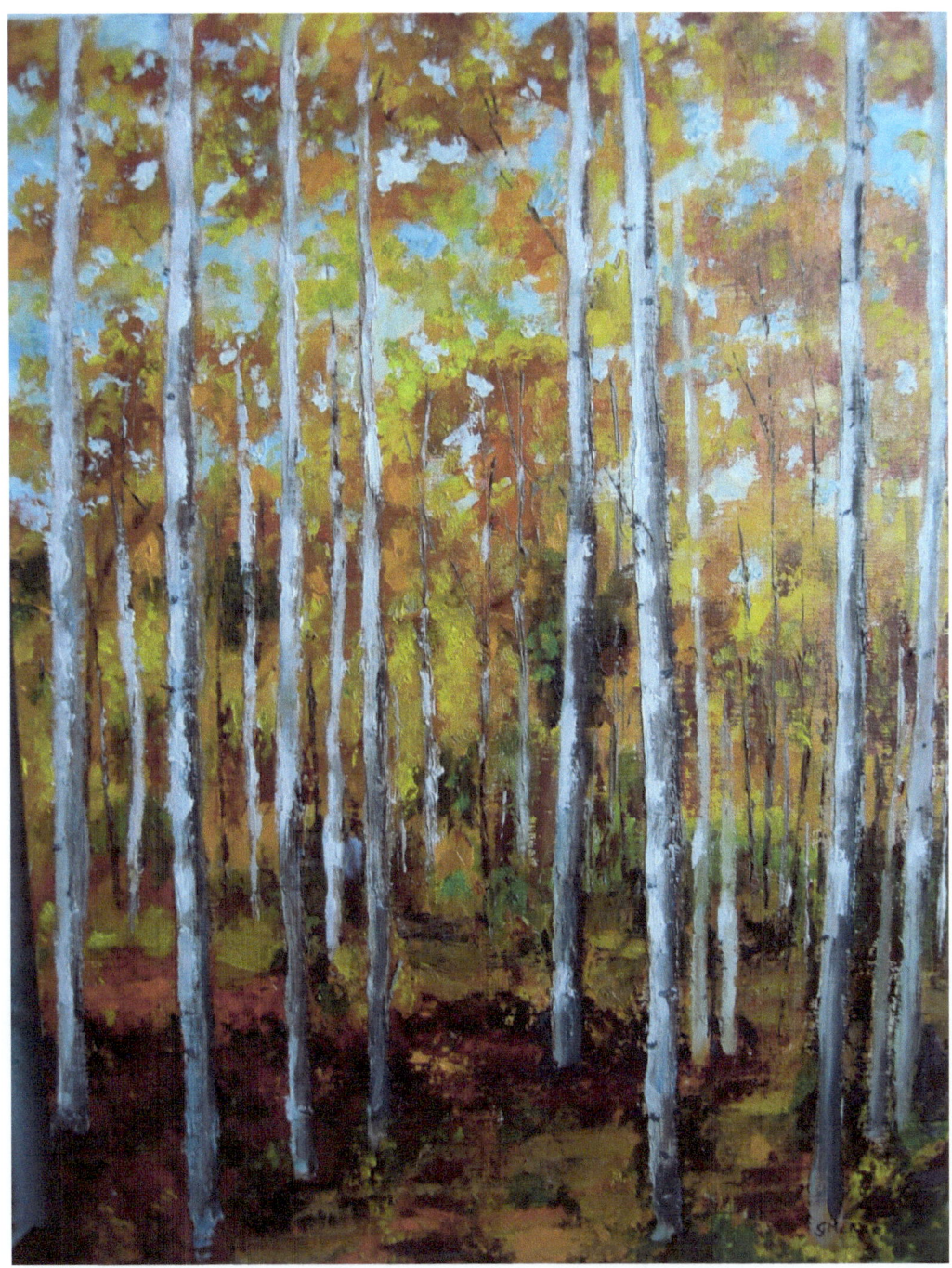

THE MYSTERIOUS WOOD

This wonderful wood in one of the northeastern states in the United States looked quite mysterious and scary on a cold foggy autumnal day. I was happy to photograph it to paint later in my studio but there was no way that I was going to venture deeper into that wood. Ghosts and hobgoblins might have been lurking there!

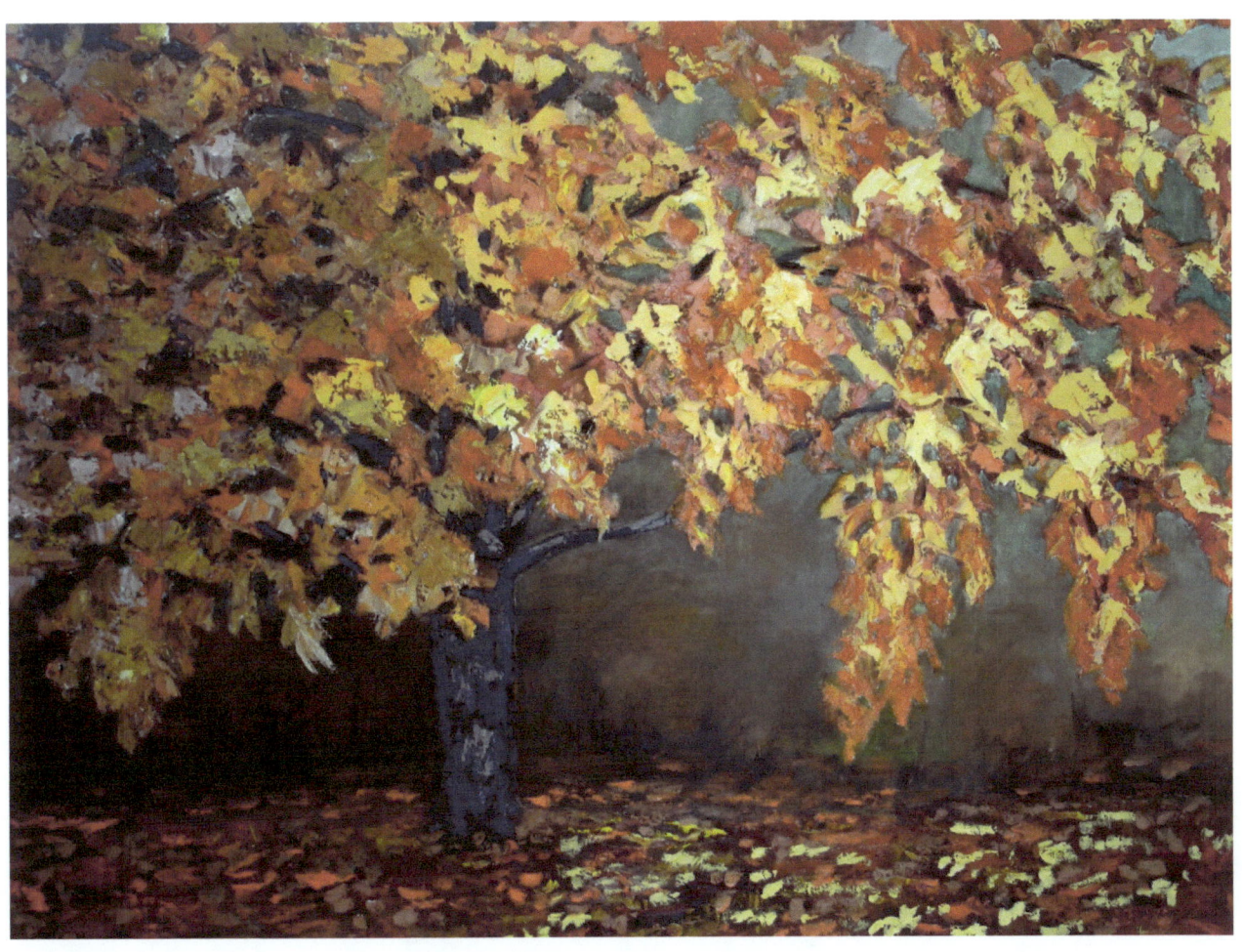

SHADES OF AUTUMN

Fall in New England is a beautiful blaze of colour! The trees display glorious yellow, red, scarlet and russet colours before the leaves eventually fall.

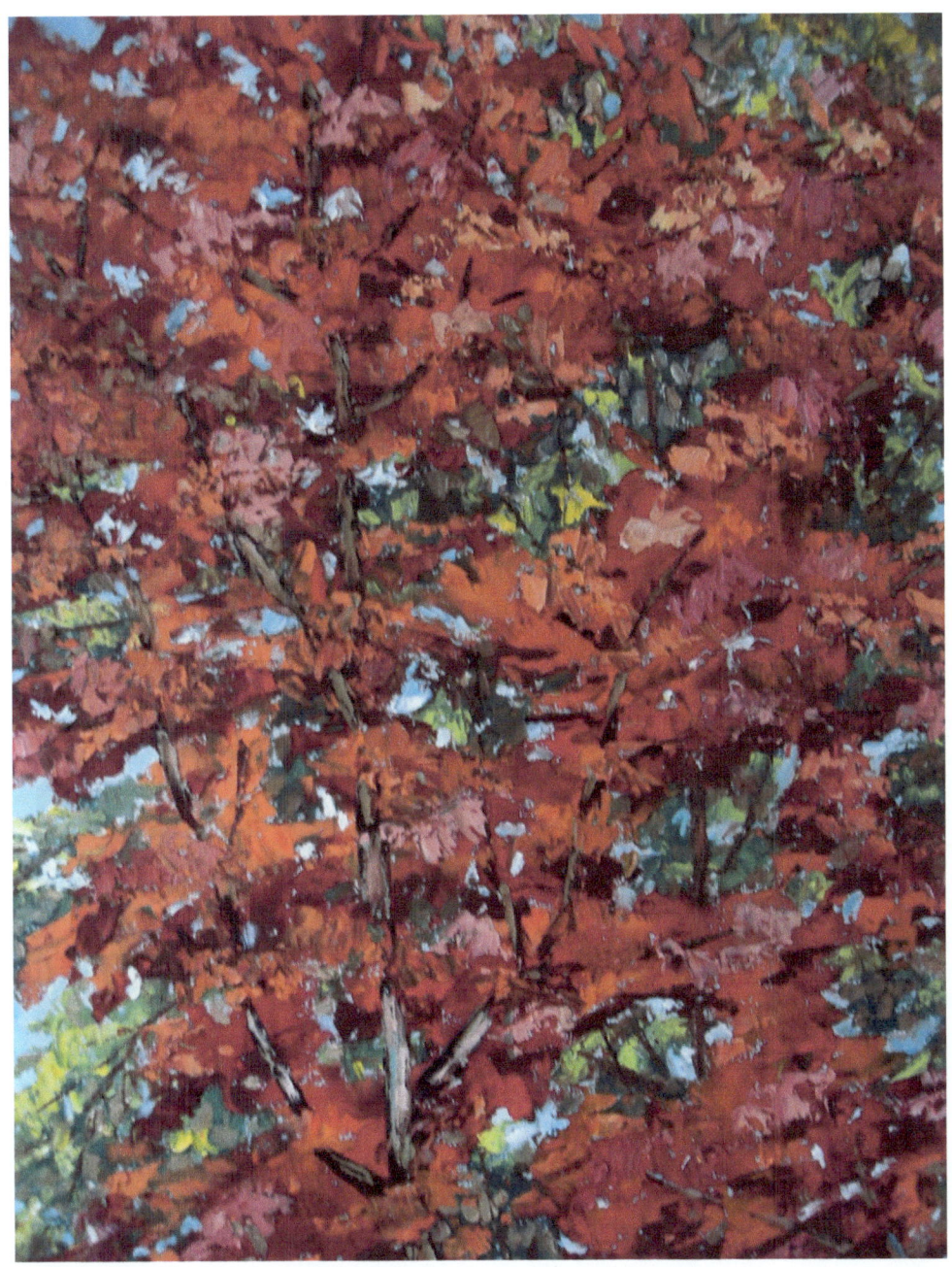

TOWER BRIDGE

Tower Bridge in London is much more spectacular at night when it is all lit up. The reflections in the water caught my eye and just begged to be painted.

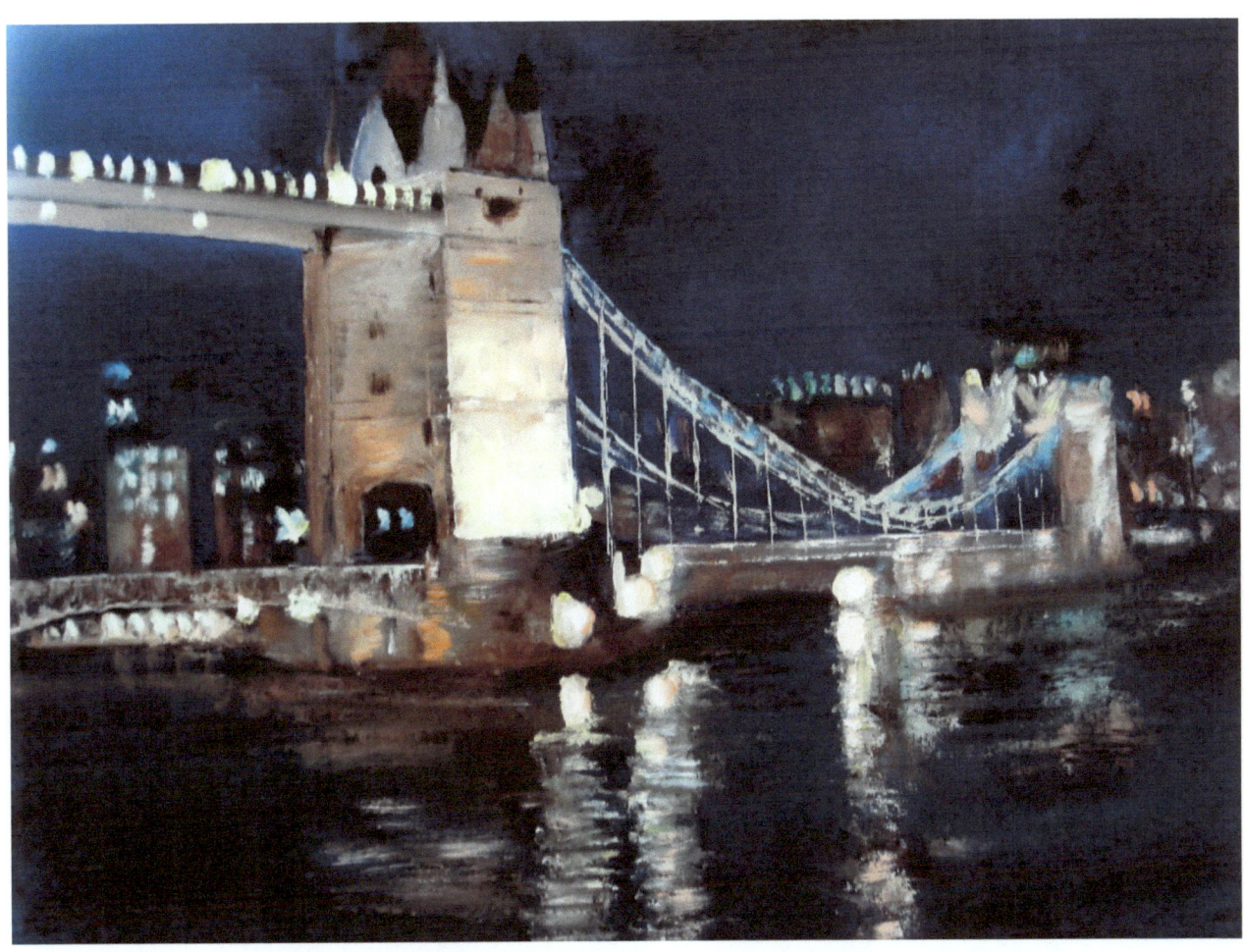

LADIES VIEW, KILLARNEY

Ireland is full of scenic beauty. This is an unforgettable view that just had to be painted!

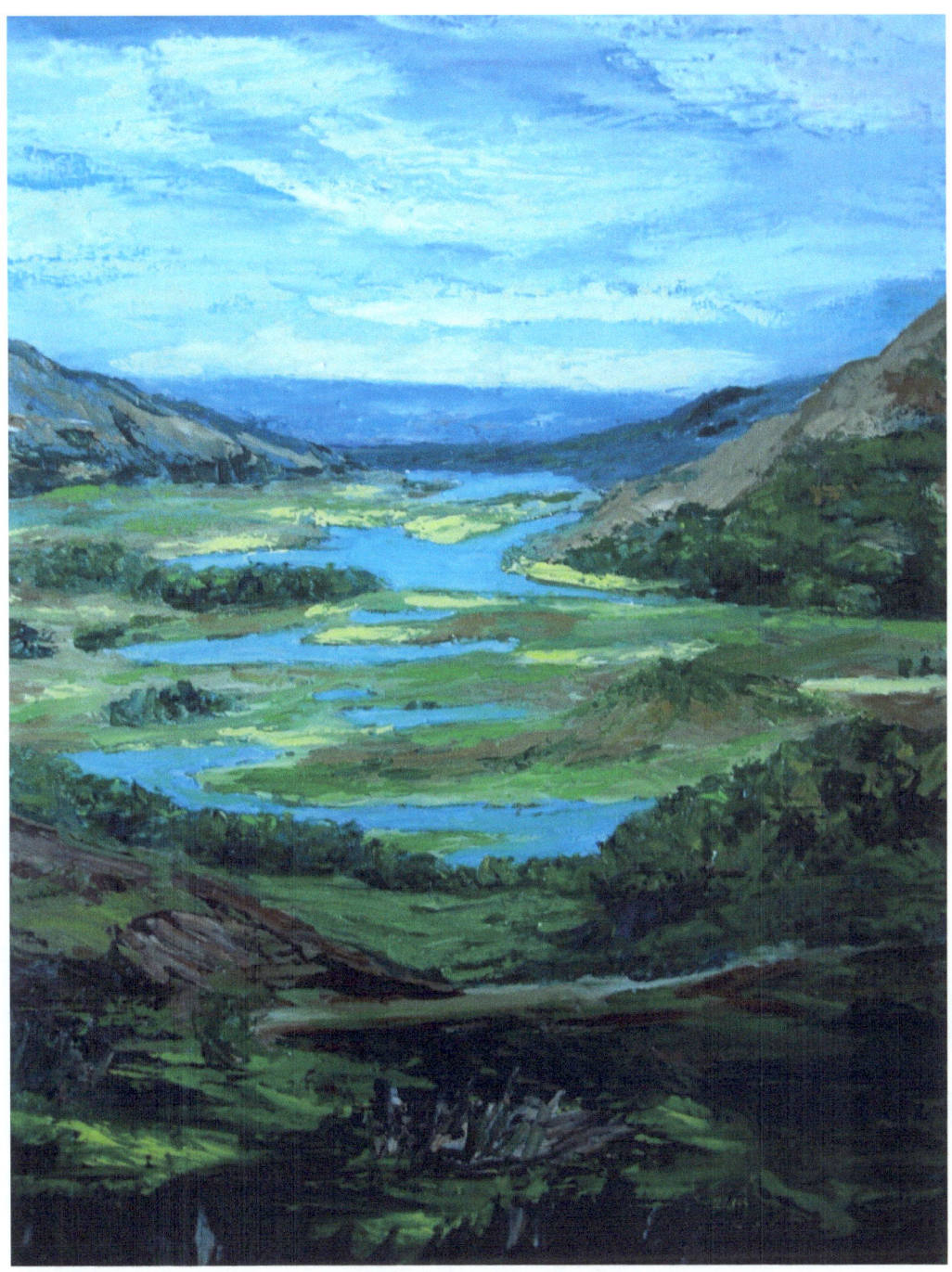

ON THE XOCHIMILCO RIVER

Mexico City is colourful, noisy and bustling, with street stalls and throngs of people in brightly coloured clothes. One highlight of our trip was a boat ride on the Xochimilco River. It was packed with boats painted in brilliant hues, some crammed with people singing, others with vendors selling all kinds of food and crafts. There were beautiful garden centres along the banks interspersed with quiet spaces with homes and moored boats.

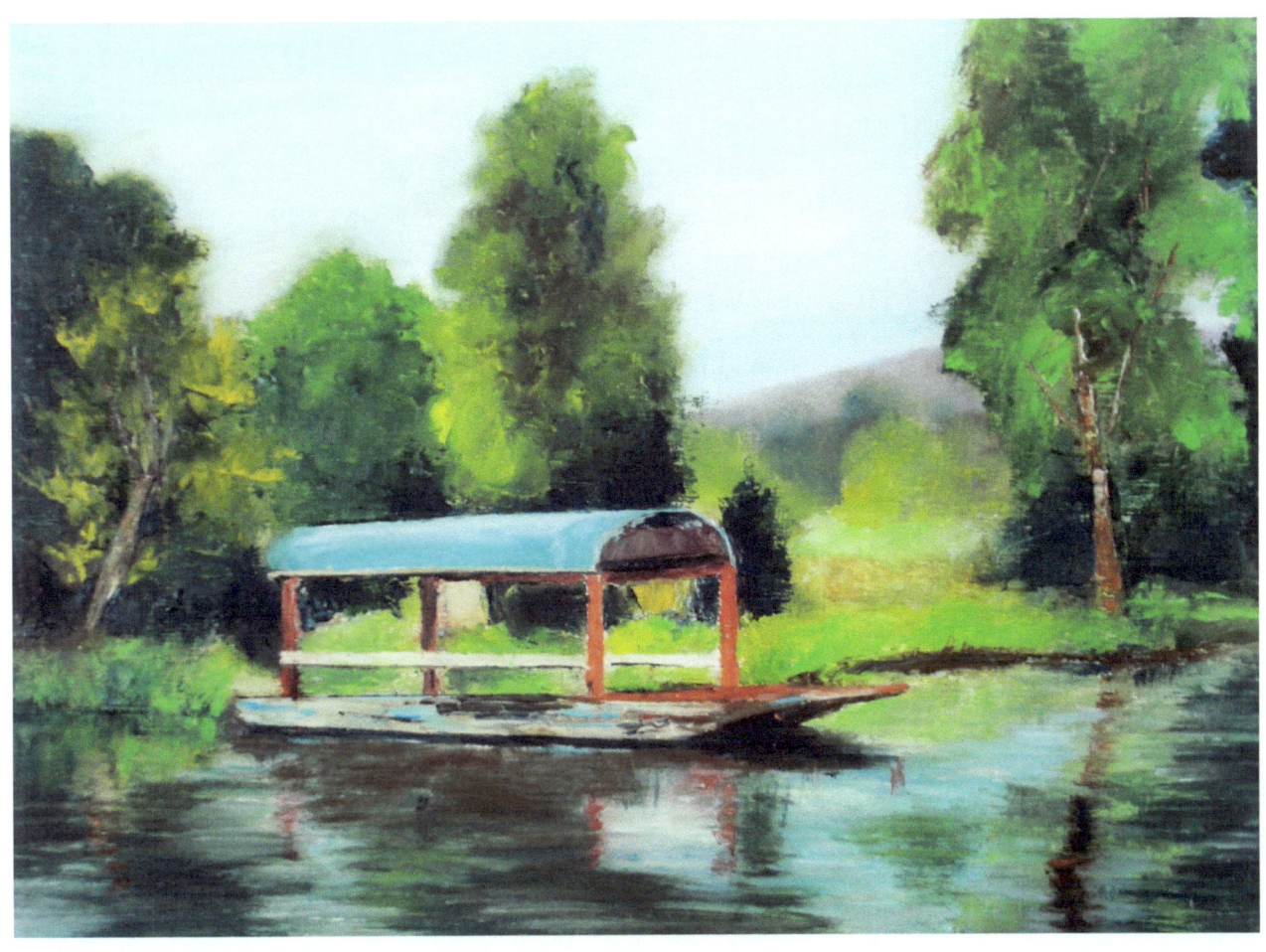

STILL LIFE WITH BOTTLE AND FRUIT

There is much beauty in ordinary household objects and fruit always adds a special touch to still life arrangements.

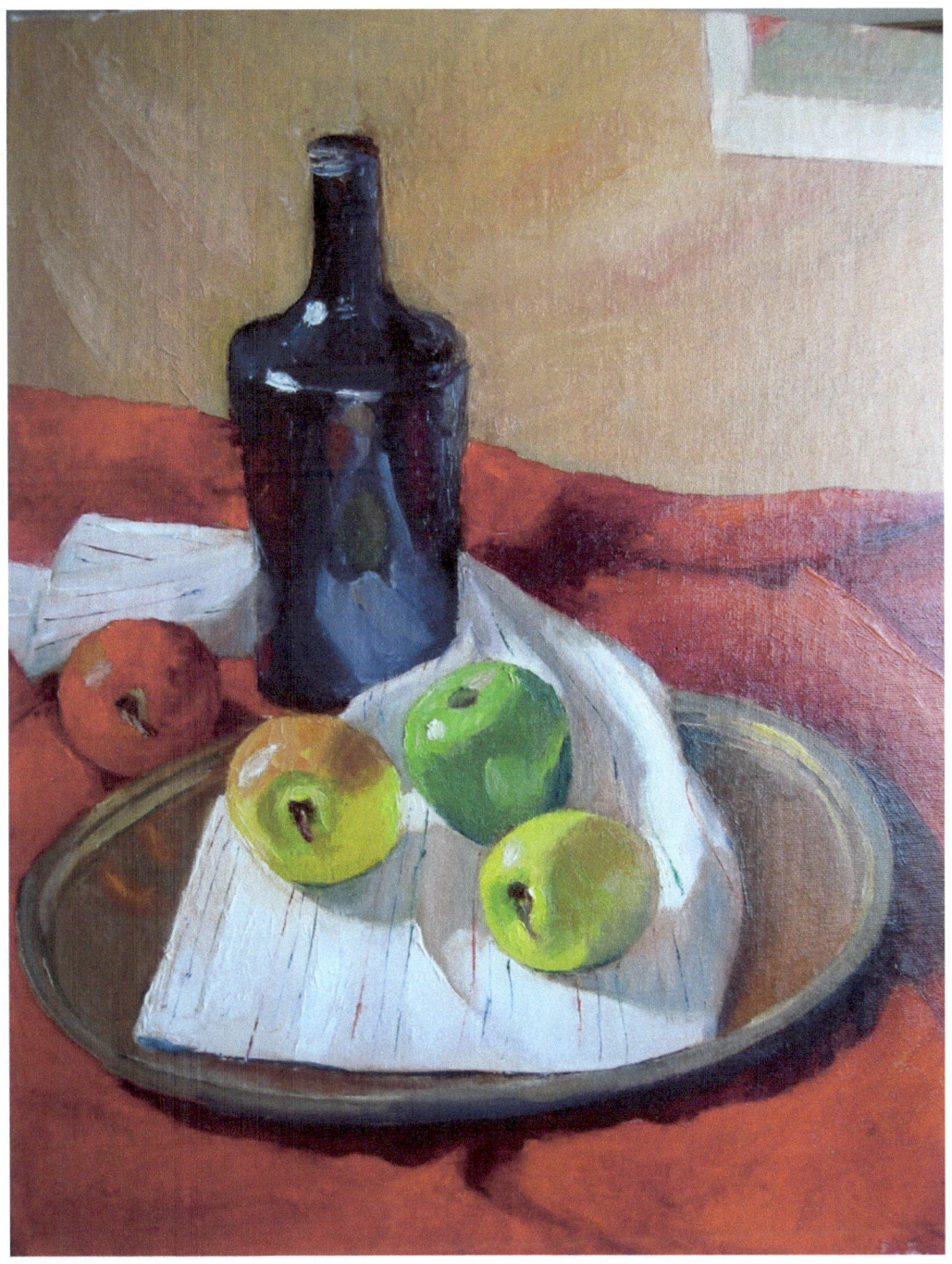

STILL LIFE WITH BUCKET AND FRUIT

An old rusted bucket, a bottle and small box with some fruit make an interesting display.

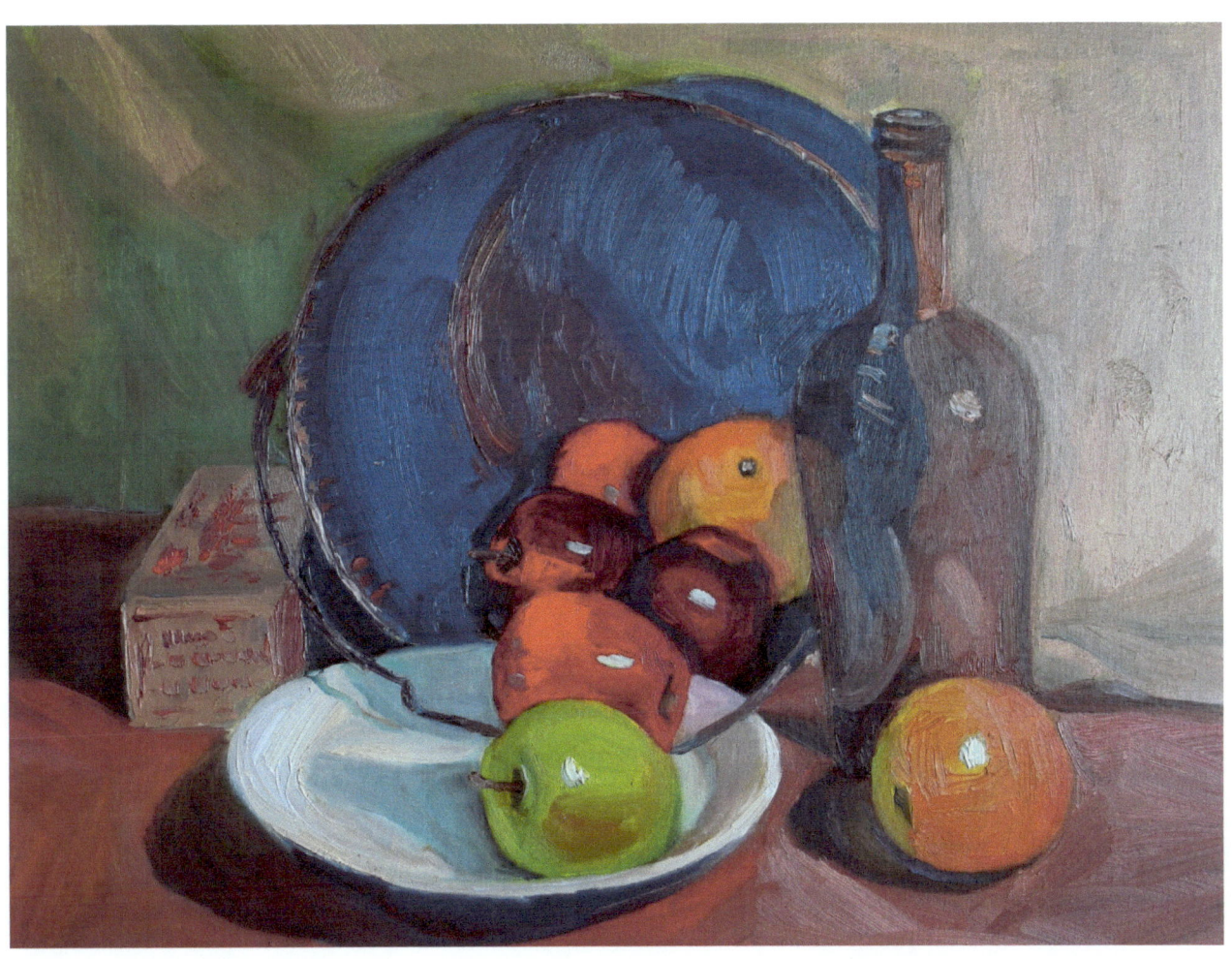

STILL LIFE WITH COPPER BOWL

This is one of my favourite paintings because it was such fun painting the copper bowl with the orange nestled in it.

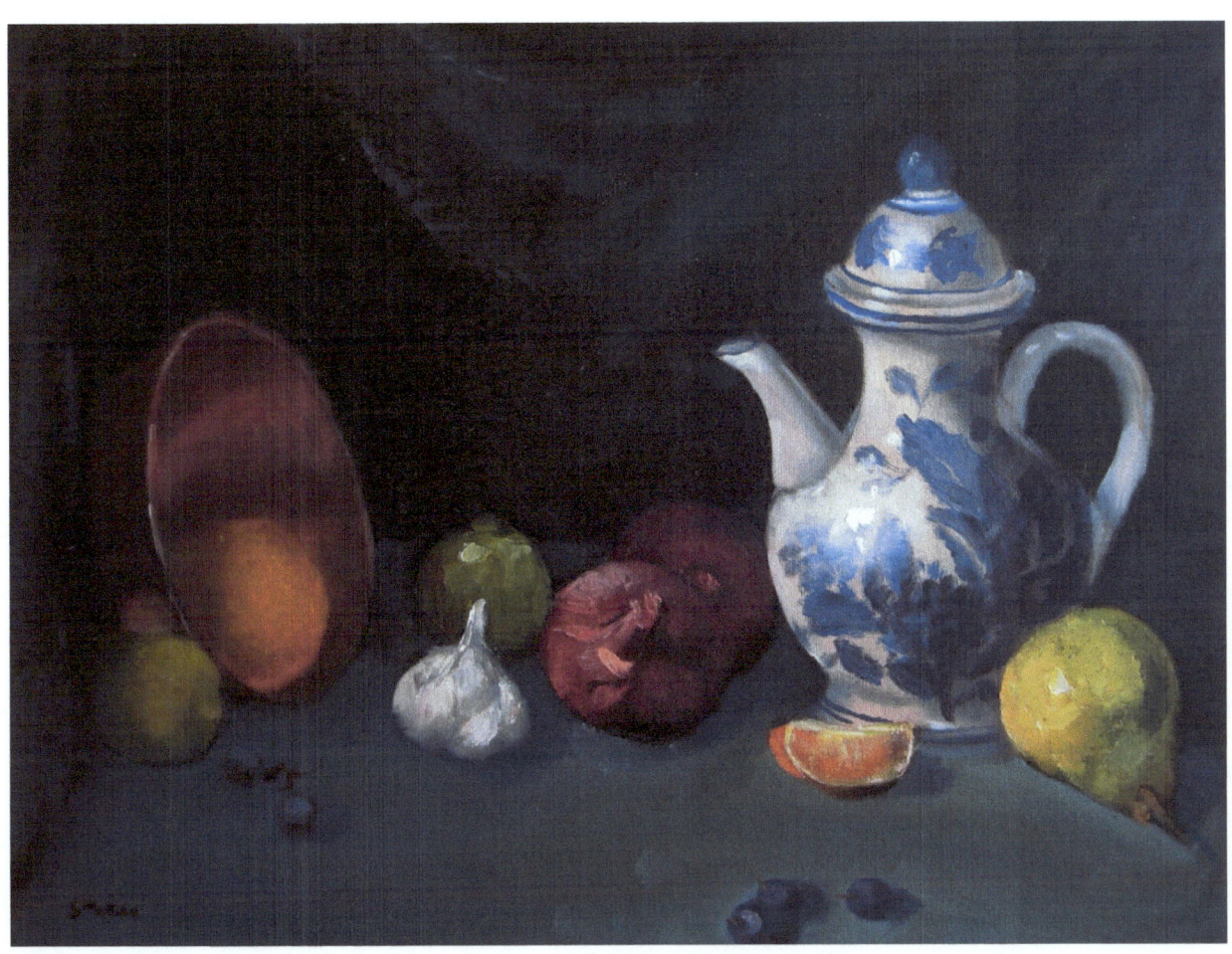

COPPER KETTLE WITH ORANGES

Reflections of oranges in a copper kettle – so beautiful!

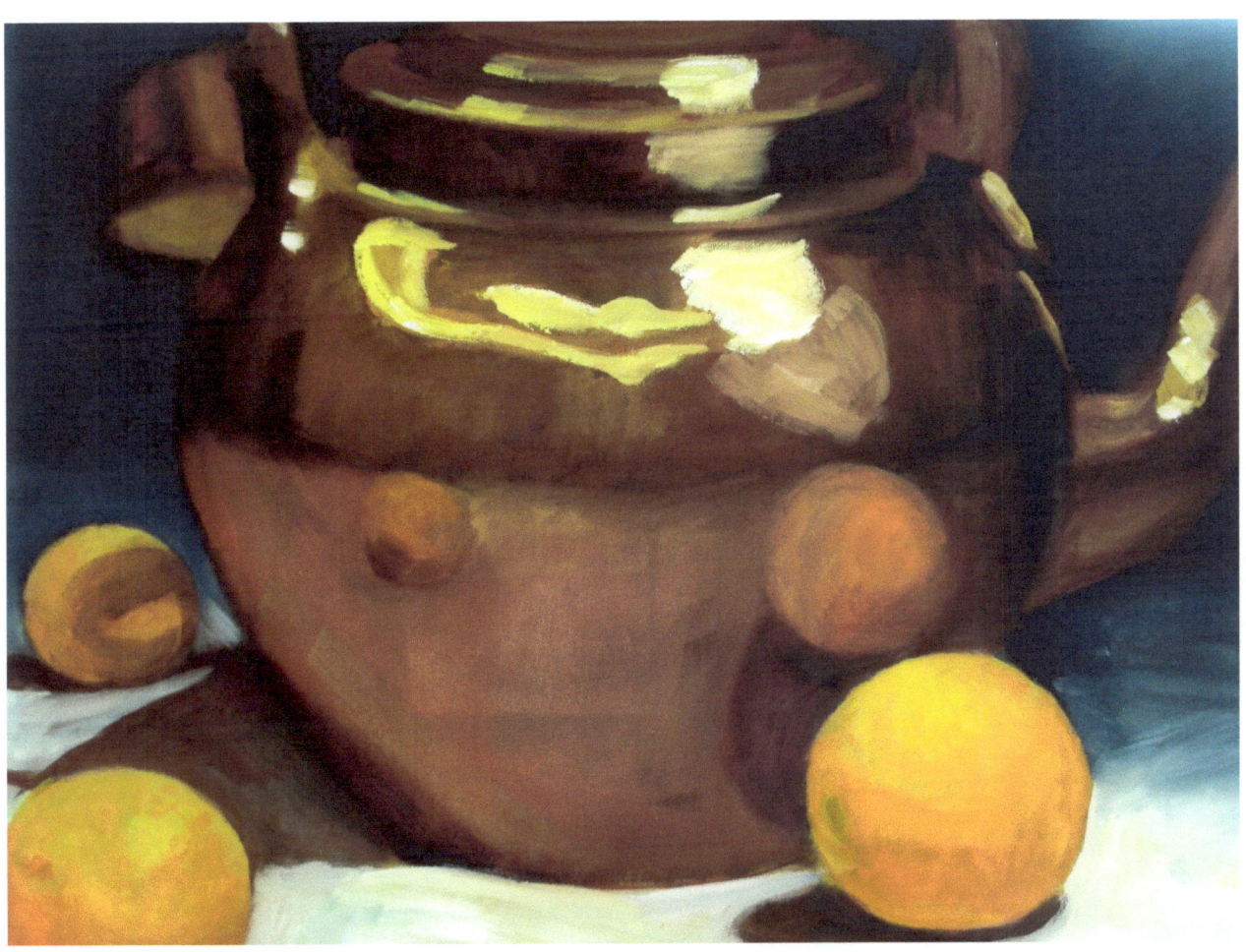

STILL LIFE WITH FRUIT AND VEGETABLES

There is so much beauty in the brilliant colours and beautiful shapes of ordinary foods when we look at them as subjects for a painting.

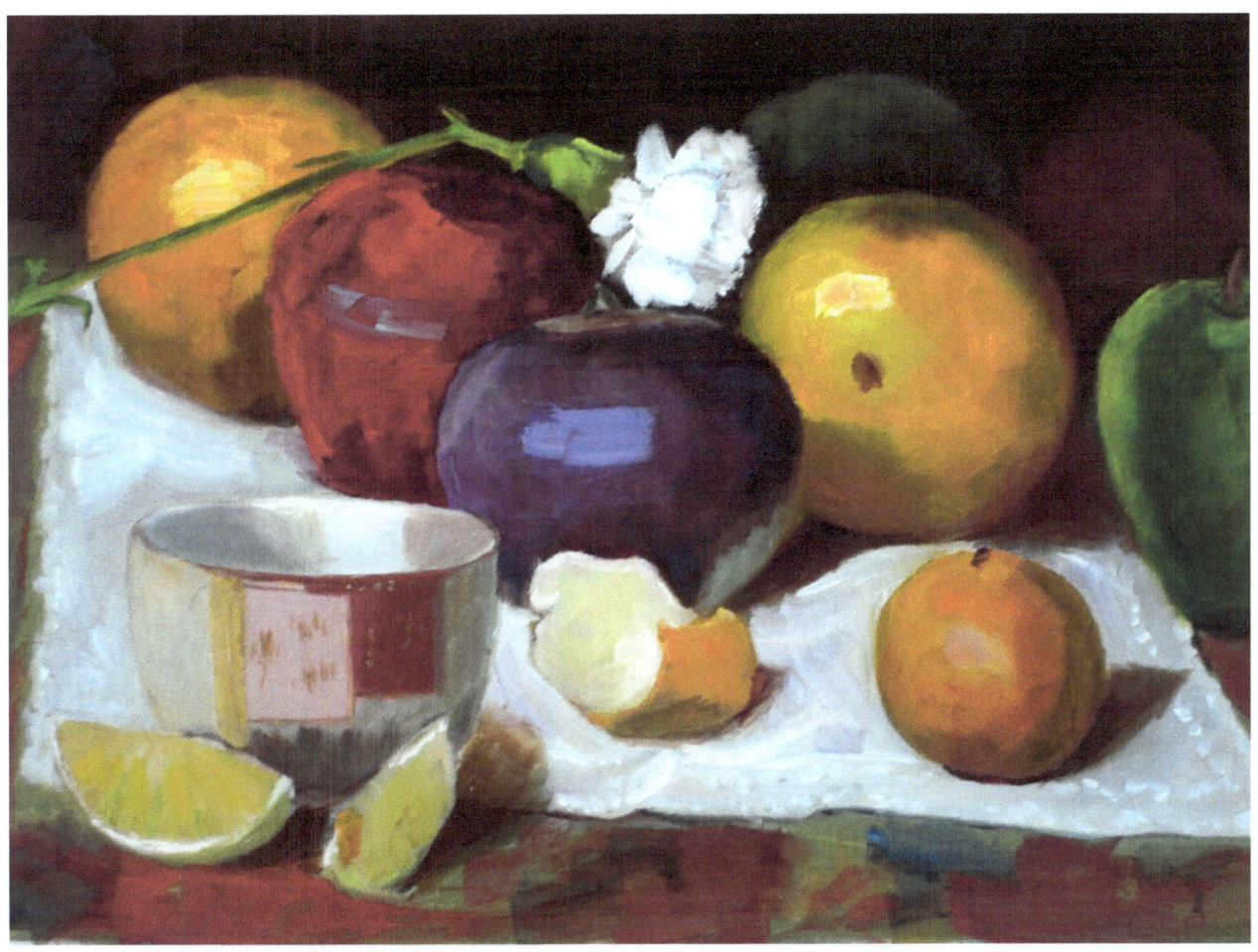

BREAKFAST ANYONE?

Special breed chickens laid these colourful eggs. The colour variations made them all the more interesting to paint.

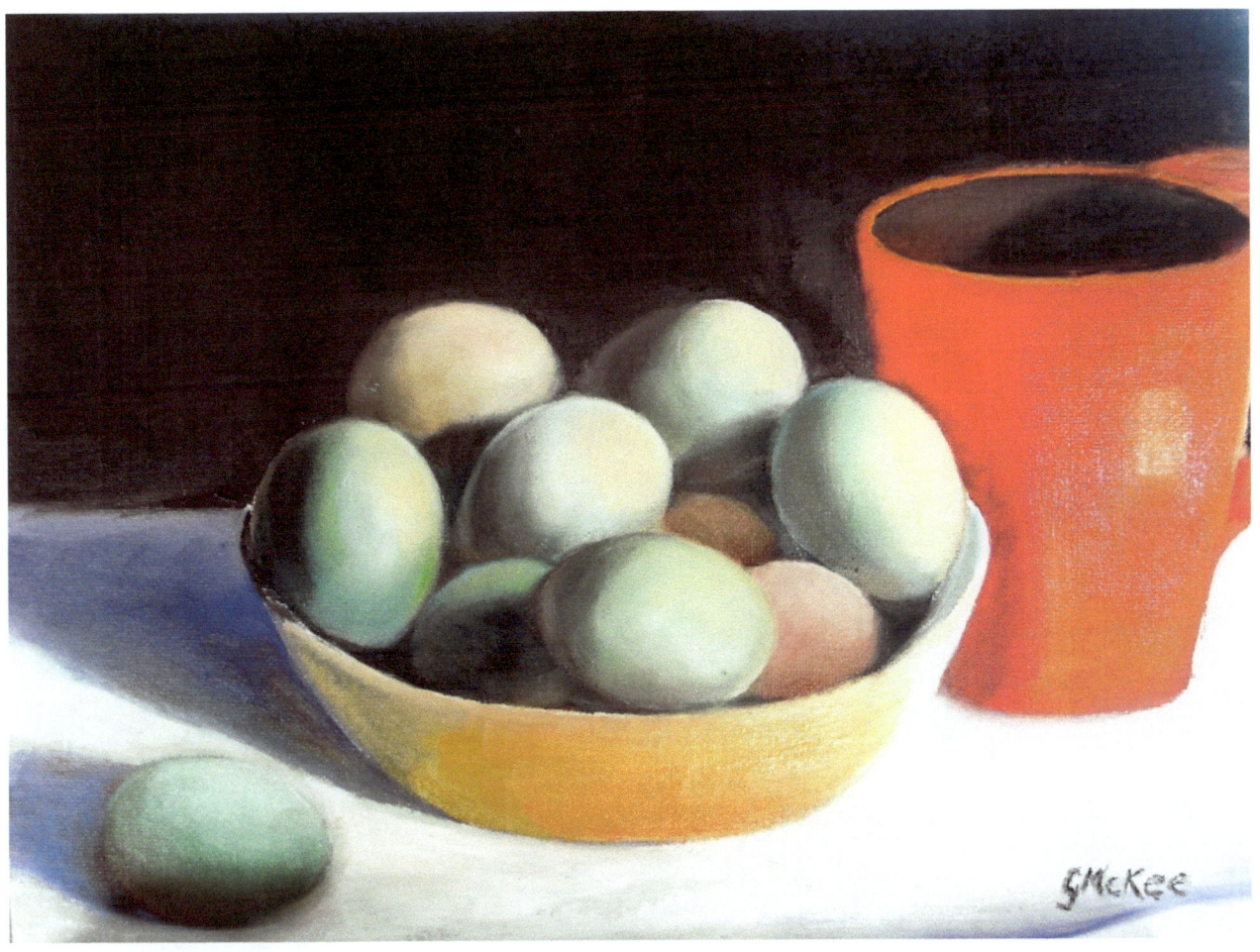

CHILLI PEPPERS

Here we have a colourful array of peppers and hot chillies of various shapes and sizes, ranging from green and yellow to red.

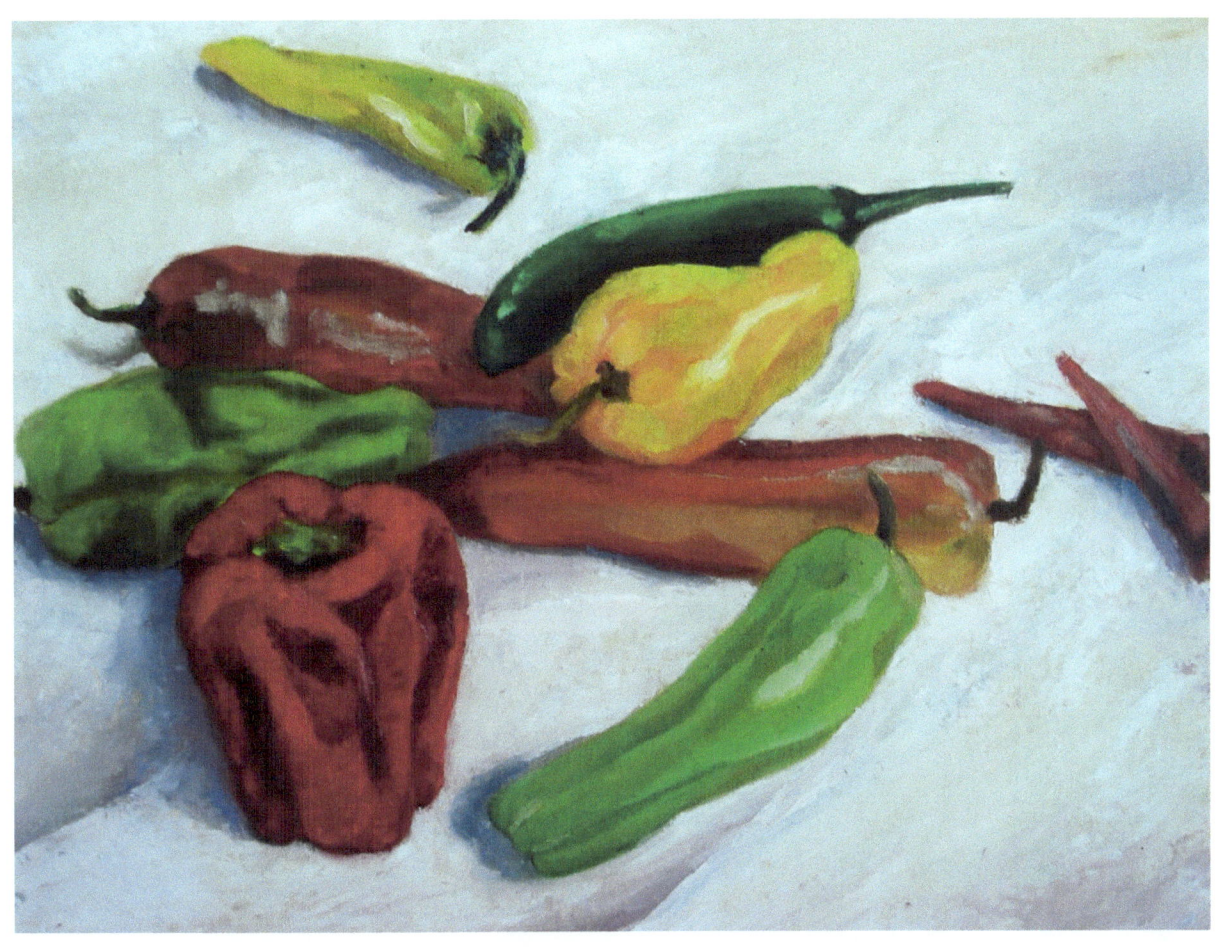

TUSCAN DEMIJOHNS

I fell in love with these huge glass bottles on a recent visit to Tuscany. They were used many years ago to store wine and old homes still have demijohns lying unused in their barns. The bottles are all slightly irregular in shape and are of different sizes and varying shades of green.

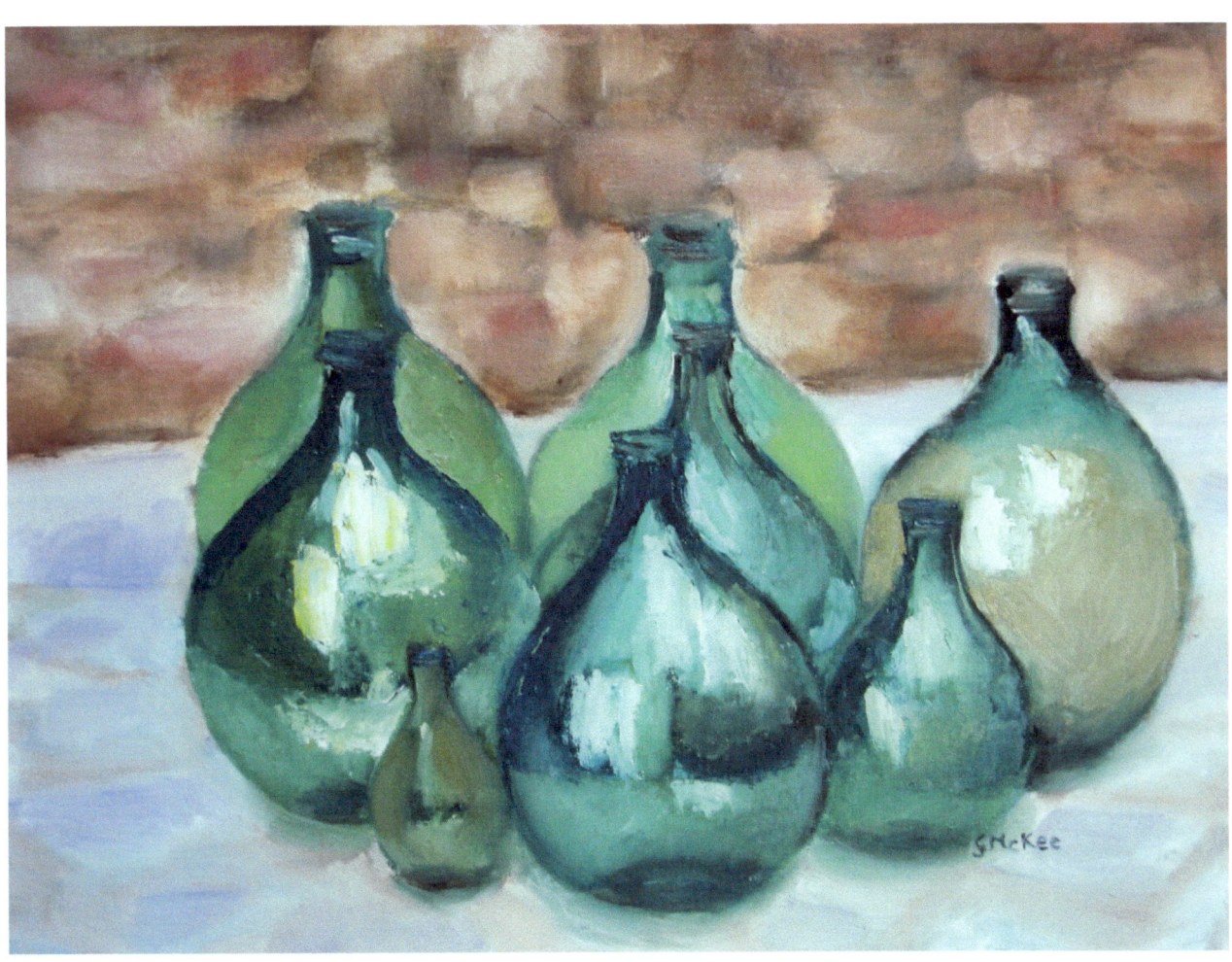

STILL LIFE WITH DRAGON AND BOWL

A green ceramic dragon, a beautiful blue bowl and some fruit provide colour contrasts as well as interesting shadows.

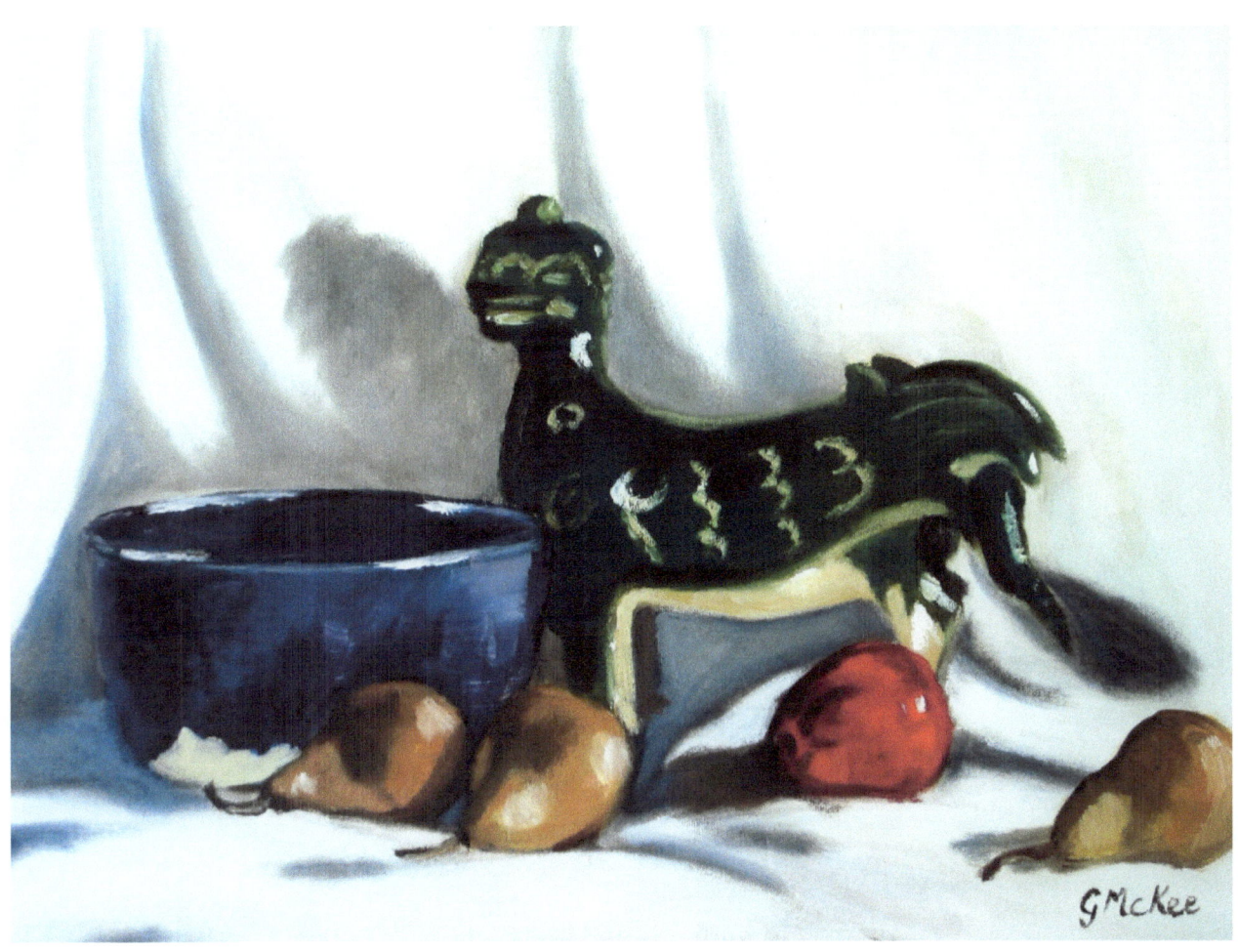

AGAINST RED SILK

Portraits are interesting to paint especially when there are subtle colour changes such as the red silk backdrop that is reflected in this young lady's face.

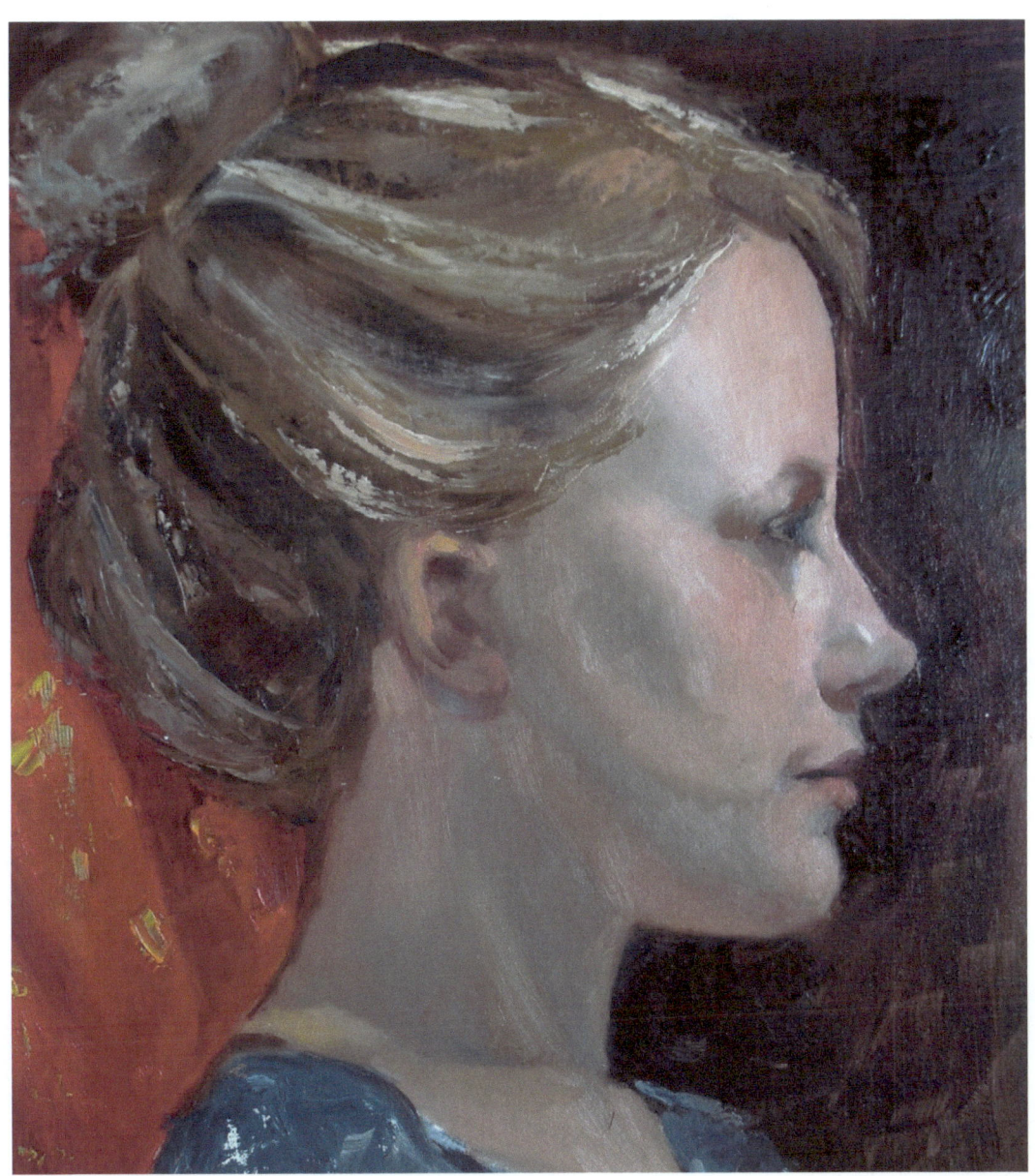

FRENCH POPPIES

Poppies are beautiful flowers, usually seen in every shade of orange, red and pink. Their crinkly petals are a challenge to paint. I find the brilliance of the bright orange ones irresistible.

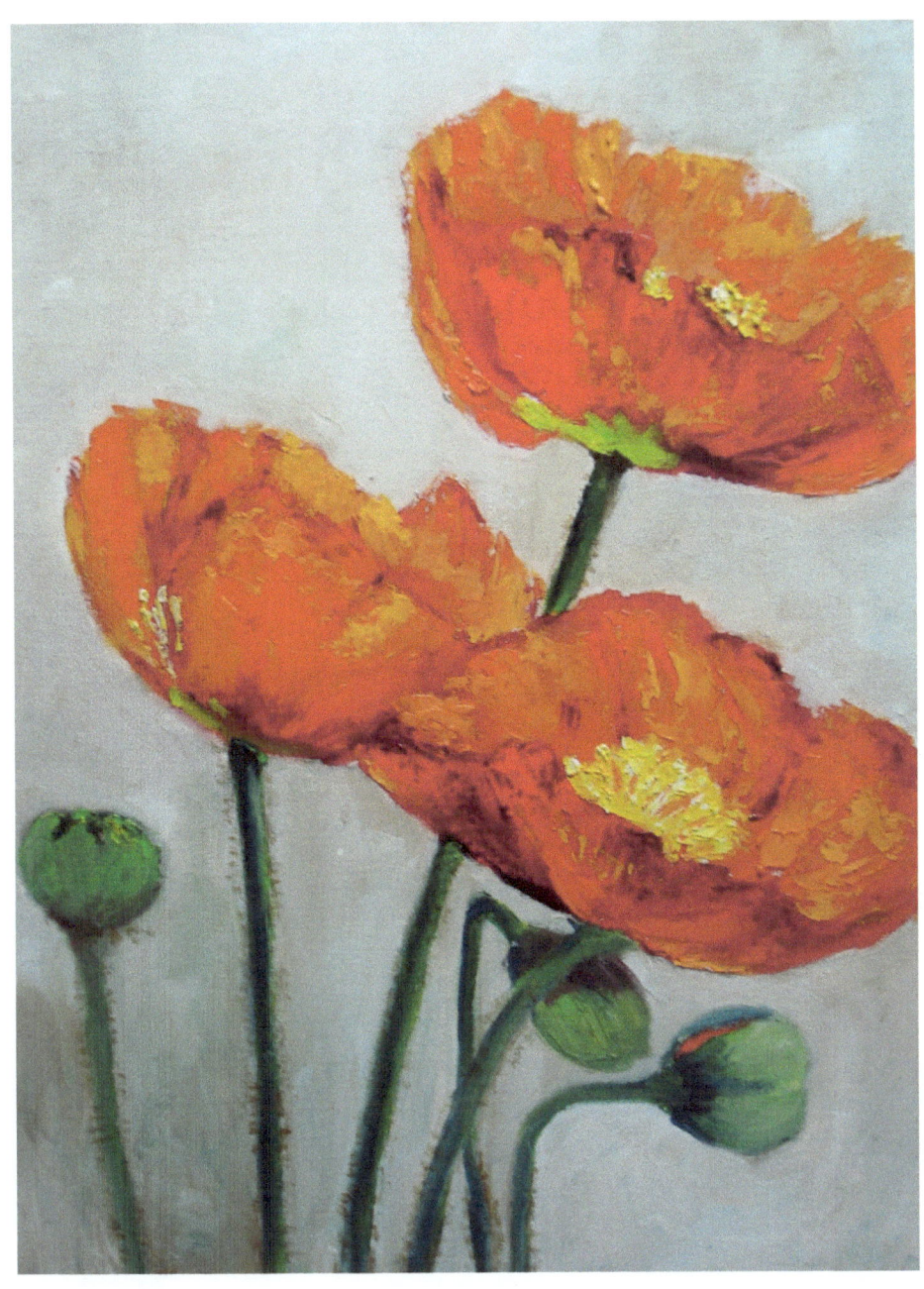

WHITE ORCHIDS

Orchids can be quite flamboyant.   Even the white ones show beautiful shades of pink and crimson within.

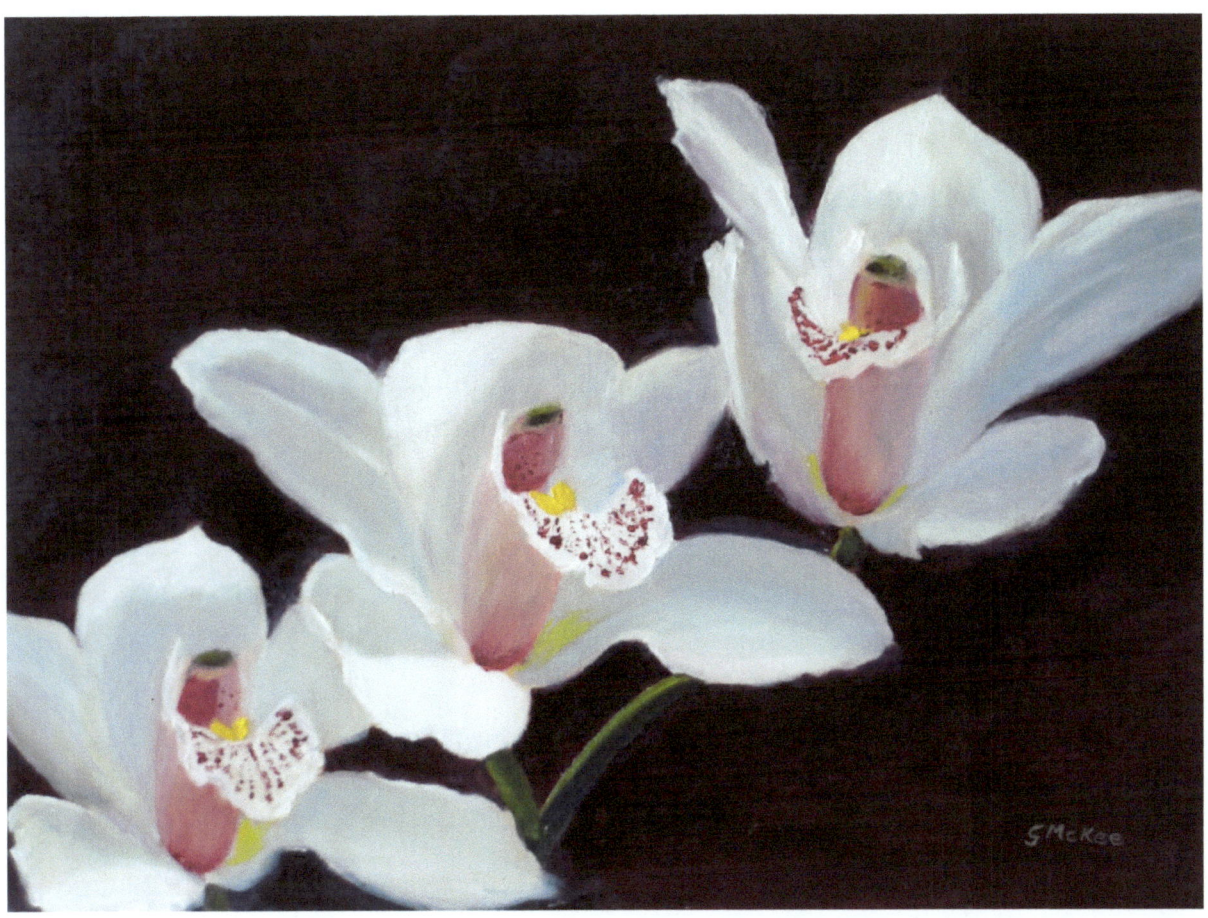

LOREE'S IRISES

A close friend and neighbour in Sedona presented me with some purple irises from her garden. Naturally I had to paint them.

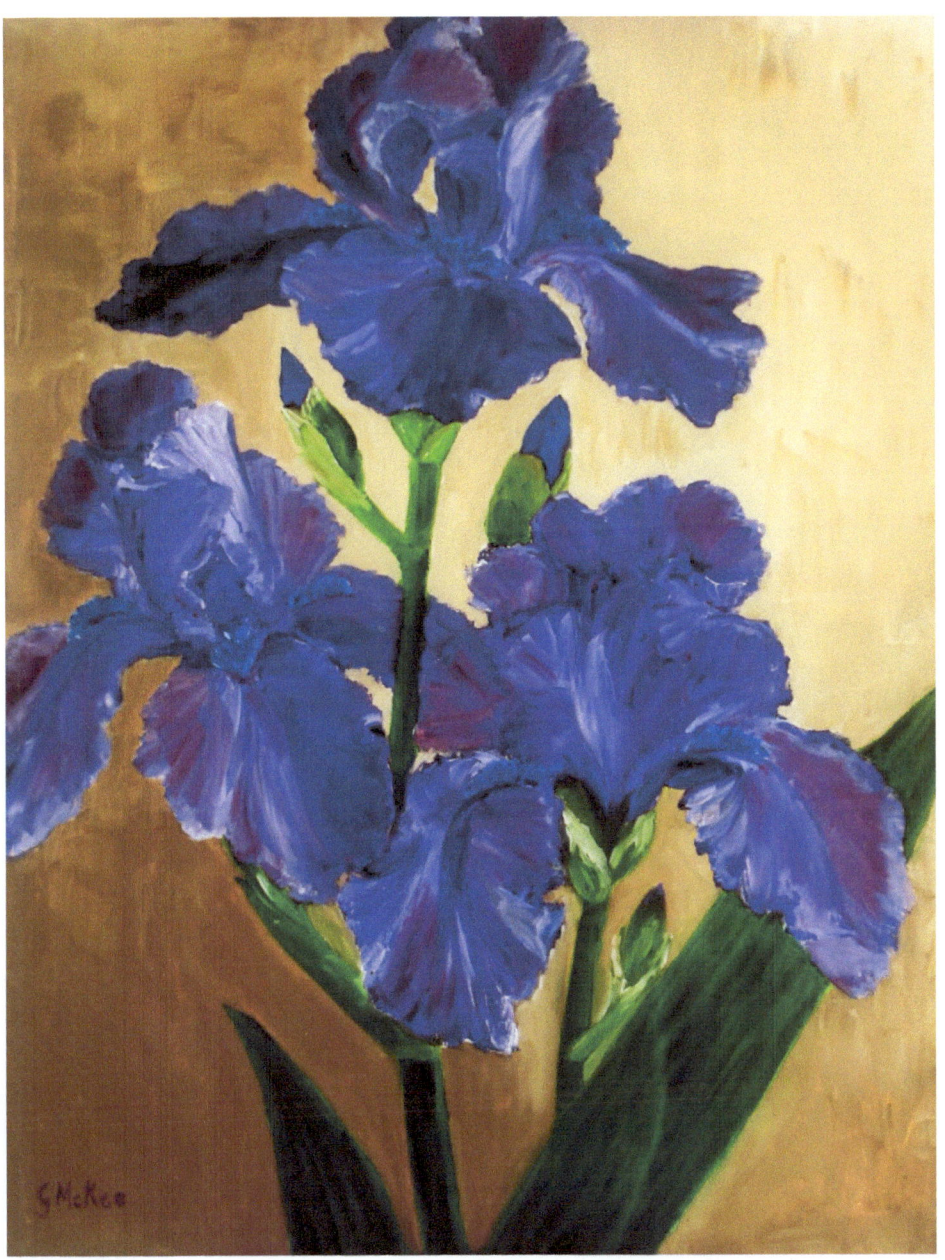

YELLOW AND WHITE POPPIES

The delicate crinkly petals of yellow and white poppies are highlighted in this watercolour painting.

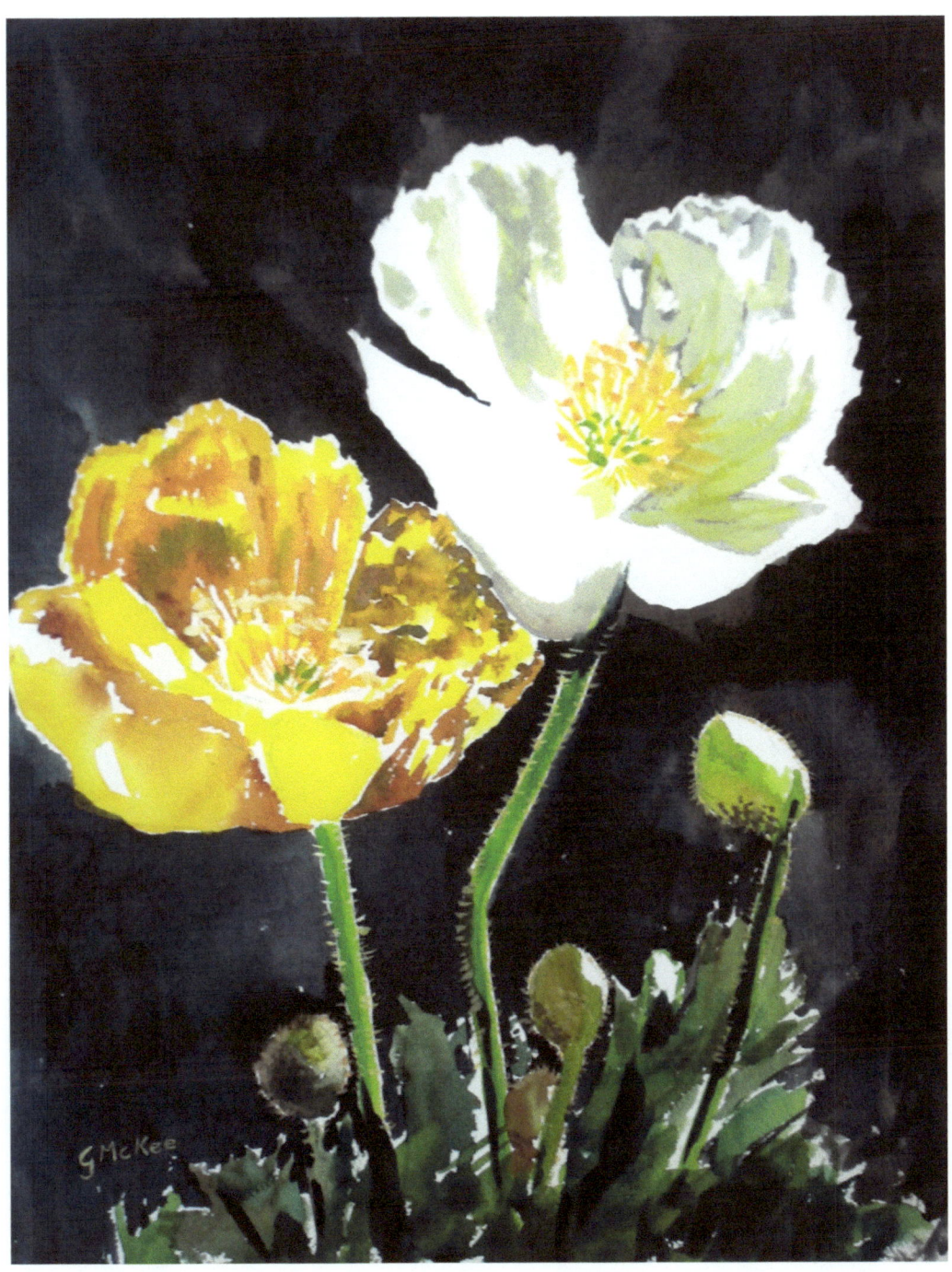

www.ingramcontent.com/pod-product-compliance
Lightning Source LLC
Chambersburg PA
CBHW050740180526
45159CB00003B/1294